THE MURDER OF JONBENÉT RAMSEY

BY RACHEL BITHELL

AMERICAN CRIME STORIES

Essential Library

An Imprint of Abdo Publishing | abdobooks.com

Cover Photos: David Zalubowski/AP Images (house); Wikimedia Commons (note)
Interior Photos: Globe Photos/Zuma Press, Inc./Alamy, 5; Red Line Editorial, 7; Steven D Starr/Corbis Historical/Getty, 10, 48; Wikimedia Commons, 13; David Zalubowski/AP Images, 17, 37; Donated to the Denver Public Library by the Rocky Mountain News, 19, 47, 67, 71, 83, 87, 97; Cliff Grassmick/Digital First Media/Boulder Daily Camera/MediaNews Group/Getty, 20; Joe Mahoney/AP Images, 23; Laura Farr/AdMedia/Newscom, 27; Michael Smith/Newsmakers/Hulton Archive/Getty, 31, 33; Donated to the Denver Public Library by the Rocky Mountain News/Linda McConnell, 39; Mario Tama/AFP/Getty, 44; Axel Koester/Sygma/Getty, 51; Chris Rank/AP Images, 53; Helen H. Richardson/Denver Post/Getty, 55; Jack Dempsey/AP Images, 58; Mark Leffingwell/AFP/Getty, 61; Donated to the Denver Public Library by the Rocky Mountain News/Ahmad Terry, 63; Alexander James Towle/Fairfax Media Archives/Getty, 68; Chris Rank/Sygma/Getty, 73; Denver Post/Getty, 75; Tony Esparza/CBS/Getty, 77; Donated to the Denver Public Library by the Rocky Mountain News/Ellen Jaskol, 78; Rick Maiman/Sygma/Getty, 80; Donated to the Denver Public Library by the Rocky Mountain News/Barry Gutierrez, 84; Paul Aiken/Digital First Media/Boulder Daily Camera/MediaNews Group/Getty, 89; Saeed Khan/AFP/Getty, 91; Donna Svennevik/Disney General Entertainment Content/Getty, 93

Editor: Christa Kelly
Series Designer: Melissa Martin

Library of Congress Control Number: 2023939443

PUBLISHER'S CATALOGING-IN-PUBLICATION DATA

Names: Bithell, Rachel, author.
Title: The murder of JonBenét Ramsey / by Rachel Bithell
Description: Minneapolis, Minnesota: Abdo Publishing, 2024 | Series: American crime stories | Includes online resources and index.
Identifiers: ISBN 9781098292126 (lib. bdg.) | ISBN 9798384910060 (ebook)
Subjects: LCSH: Crime and criminals--Juvenile literature. | Killing (Murder)--Juvenile literature. | United States--Juvenile literature. | Ramsey, JonBenét, 1990-1996--Juvenile literature. | Beauty contestants--Crimes against--Juvenile literature. | Colorado--Boulder--Juvenile literature. | Children--Crimes against--Juvenile literature.
Classification: DDC 364.97--dc23

CONTENTS

This book discusses accounts of crime, violence, and death that may be disturbing to some readers.

FROM MISSING TO MURDERED

t 5:52 a.m. on December 26, 1996, police received a frantic 911 call.

"We have a kidnapping!" a woman said, out of breath. "Hurry, please!"

"Explain to me what is going on, OK?" the operator said.

"Our daughter is gone!"[1]

Within minutes, police arrived. It would take them hours to find the body of the missing little girl. It would take them years more to sort through the evidence. Decades later, the mystery remains: Who killed JonBenét Ramsey?

JonBenét's Final Christmas

In December 1996, the Ramsey family had much to celebrate. After nearly two years, an extensive renovation of their 1927

JonBenét was the youngest child of John and Patsy Ramsey.

home in Boulder, Colorado, was finally complete, just in time for the holidays. The Ramsey children, JonBenét, age six, and her brother Burke, age nine, were especially excited about their newly decorated bedrooms. Their parents, John and Patsy, were relieved that the renovations were over. They were tired of having dozens of workers coming and going through their house and were looking forward to relaxing in their beautiful home. With windows looking onto the gorgeous Flatirons, a stretch of sweeping sandstone peaks, the Boulder home would be the perfect place to celebrate Christmas.

Patsy had begun the holiday season by lavishly decorating their large house. She and her children put up dozens of decorations, many from a previous Christmas when their house was featured in a holiday tour of historic homes.

"I overdid the decorations. I know I did," said Patsy later. "But it was part of living in the moment."[2] Patsy had learned to make every moment count. She had been diagnosed with

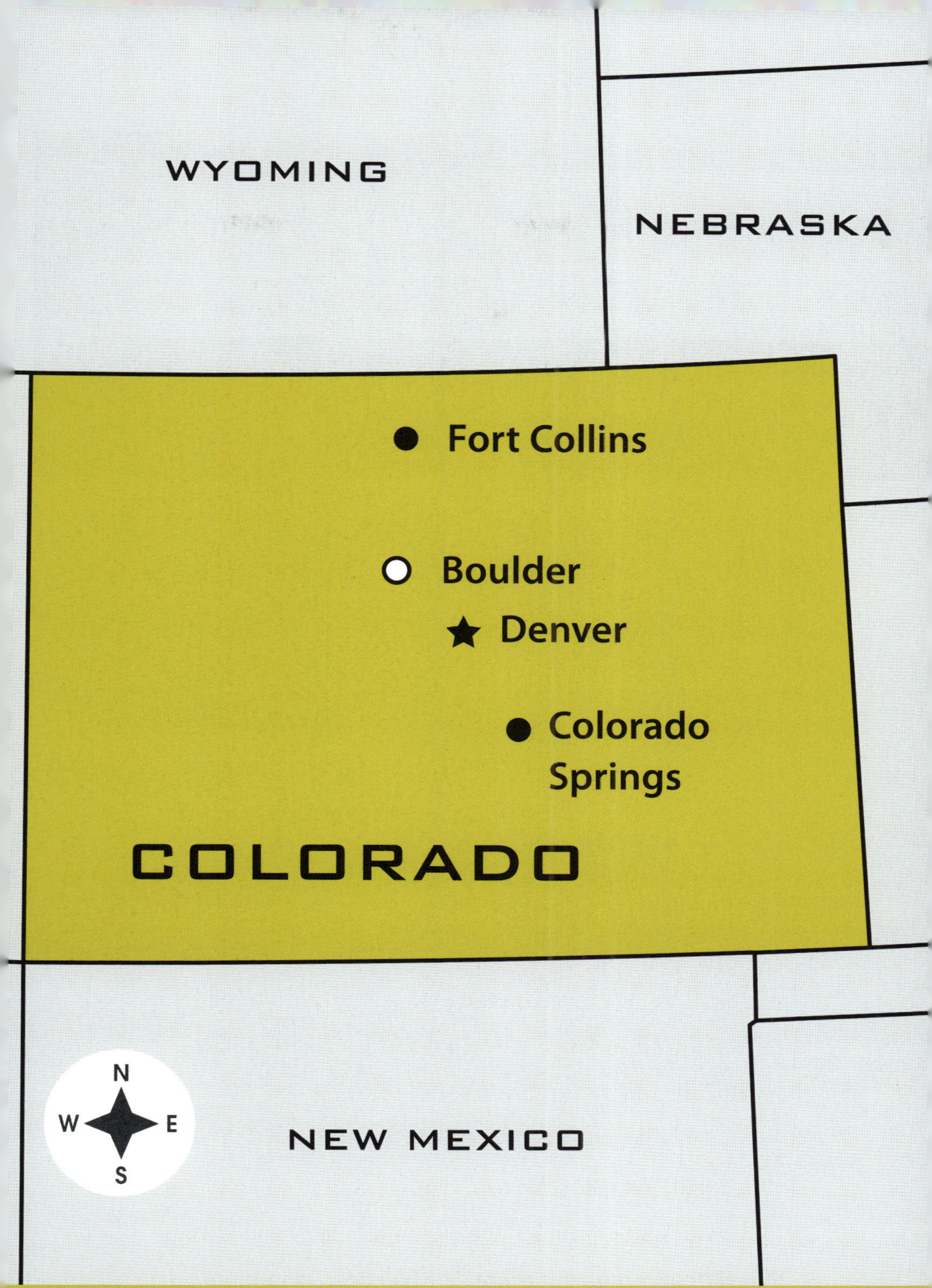

The Ramsey family lived in Boulder, an affluent city in Colorado.

John Ramsey's career brought the Ramsey family to Boulder in 1991. They purchased their home at 755 15th Street for $500,000. The day of JonBenét's death, they left the home and never spent another night there. In 1998, a group of investors bought the home for $650,000. They sold it to a family in 2004 for $1.05 million. The house's number was changed, but the home's history still made it difficult to sell. It was listed for sale in 2008, 2009, 2011, and 2014 with no buyers. In March 2023, it hit the market again with an asking price of $6.95 million.[5]

stage 4 ovarian cancer in 1993. Doctors said her chances of survival were slim. Clinging to hope, she commuted to Maryland for months for an experimental treatment that included major surgery and chemotherapy. In 1994, she was pronounced cancer-free, and now, two years later, she was grateful to still be in remission.

On December 6, Burke and JonBenét participated in the ninth annual Boulder Parade of Lights. JonBenét rode in a red convertible wearing a crown and sash, trophies from a beauty pageant she'd competed in. She smiled and waved to the crowd watching the parade, nestled next to three other young beauty queens. But she was jealous that Burke, marching with his Boy Scout troop, would be the one throwing out candy.

"Burke! Burke!" she called to her older brother. "Please save some for me!"[4]

The Ramseys were busy during the weeks leading up to Christmas, hosting and attending

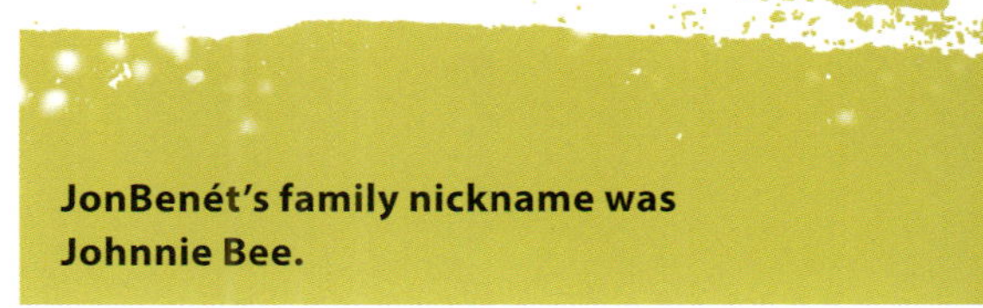

numerous parties and events. On December 15, their church congregation gathered for a Christmas party at the Ramseys' home. On December 17, JonBenét entered a beauty pageant, winning the title "Colorado's Little Miss Christmas." On December 20, John's computer company, Access Graphics, held a celebration at a nearby hotel to mark hitting $1 billion in gross sales. On December 23, the Ramseys hosted a second holiday party for friends and their children, complete with an actor playing Santa Claus.

By Christmas Eve, the public festivities had died down. JonBenét and Burke went to play with friends for a few hours while their parents completed some final holiday preparations. JonBenét told her friend and her friend's mother that Santa Claus had promised her a special visit after Christmas. In the evening, the Ramsey family shook packages under the Christmas tree and read *The Night Before Christmas*. Then, JonBenét and Burke were put to bed so Santa could make his holiday visit.

JonBenét and Burke woke early on Christmas Day, and the excited children ran into their parents' bedroom at approximately 6:30 in the morning. After a Christmas breakfast

Patsy Ramsey, her children, and her housekeeper decorated the Ramseys' three-story house for Christmas, the family's favorite holiday.

of pancakes, bacon, and corned beef hash, the family spent

the morning unwrapping presents and enjoying their gifts.

JonBenét was excited to receive a new bicycle. In the afternoon,

the children played with friends in their neighborhood while

John and Patsy prepared for a trip the next day. The Ramseys

were planning to leave early on December 26 to fly to Michigan

on the family's private plane. They would spend a few days

in their vacation home with John's two adult children from a previous marriage. Then, the family planned to ring in the New Year on a Disney cruise.

That evening, the Ramseys attended a Christmas dinner party with some of their friends. On the way home, the family dropped off a few last-minute presents. JonBenét fell asleep in the car. After arriving home between 9:00 and 10:00 p.m., John carried his sleeping daughter up to her bedroom. Patsy came in a few minutes later to remove JonBenét's shoes. She left her daughter's white top in place and exchanged her pants for a pair of white long johns. With her daughter tucked in, Patsy left the sleeping girl's room. It was the last time she would see JonBenét alive.

Kidnapped?

Patsy and John woke early on December 26 to finish preparations for their trip. While John showered, Patsy headed downstairs. As she descended the spiral staircase that led to the kitchen, she noticed a few pieces of paper lying on the third step from the bottom. She picked up the paper and scanned the messy writing. Then, she screamed.

The note, addressed to John, said JonBenét had been kidnapped by a "foreign faction" and was being held for ransom.[6] It threatened to behead the girl if John failed to follow the kidnappers' instructions. Patsy read only part of the note before rushing to JonBenét's bedroom. The bed was empty.

At 5:52 a.m., Patsy called 911. As soon as she hung up the phone, she called some close friends and asked them to come to the home. At 6:00 a.m., Officer Rick French of the Boulder Police Department (BPD) arrived at the Ramsey home in a marked police car. At 6:01 a.m., the first family friends arrived. A second officer, Sergeant Paul Reichenbach, arrived one minute later.

As the first officer on the scene, French conducted a search of the home but failed to find anything significant. At about 7:00 a.m., John told Burke his sister was missing, and Burke was taken to a friend's home.

Over the next two hours, three more officers and two detectives from the BPD came to the home. When Commander-Sergeant Bob Whitson arrived at 9:00 a.m., he saw people milling throughout the house. He instructed officers to cordon off JonBenét's bedroom to prevent potential evidence from being contaminated. The investigators spent the morning lifting fingerprints from surfaces in the home. They took the ransom note into evidence and collected handwriting samples from John and Patsy.

The Ramseys and some of their friends were interviewed, but the interviews weren't recorded. The officers had brought only one tape recorder, and it was in use. They had connected it

Mr. Ramsey,

Listen carefully! We are a group of individuals that represent a small foreign faction. We respect your bussiness but not the country that it serves. At this time we have your daughter in our posession. She is safe and unharmed and if you want her to see 1997, you must follow our instructions to the letter.

You will withdraw $118,000.00 from your account. $100,000 will be in $100 bills and the remaining $18,000 in $20 bills. Make sure that you bring an adequate size attache to the bank. When you get home you will put the money in a brown paper bag. I will call you between 8 and 10 am tomorrow to instruct you on delivery. The delivery will be exhausting so I advise you to be rested. If we monitor you getting the money early, we might call you early to arrange an earlier delivery of the money and hence a earlier pick-up of your daughter.

Any deviation of my instructions will result in the immediate execution of your daughter. You will also be denied her remains for proper burial. The two gentlemen watching over your daughter do not particularly like you so I advise you not to provoke them. Speaking to anyone about your situation, such as Police, F.B.I., etc., will result in your daughter being beheaded. If we catch you talking to a stray dog, she dies. If you alert bank authorities, she dies. If the money is in any way marked or tampered with, she dies. You will be scanned for electronic devices and if any are found, she dies. You can try to deceive us but be warned that we are familiar with Law enforcement countermeasures and tactics. You stand a 99% chance of killing your daughter if you try to out smart us. Follow our instructions and you stand a 100% chance of getting her back. You and your family are under constant scrutiny as well as the authorities. Don't try to grow a brain John. You are not the only fat cat around so don't think that killing will be difficult. Don't underestimate us John. Use that good southern common sense of yours. It is up to you now John!

Victory!
S.B.T.C

The 2.5-page ransom note wasn't disclosed to the public until almost a year after JonBenét's murder.

to the home's phone in case the kidnappers called. The ransom note had promised a call with further instructions between 8:00 and 10:00 a.m.

Witnesses described Patsy that morning as "dazed" and "hysterical."[7] John was calmer but was observed pacing, crying, and praying. He made a couple of phone calls to cancel the family's travel plans and access the money demanded as ransom. Detective Linda Arndt gave John instructions as to what to say when the kidnappers called. But the phone call never came. By a few minutes after 10:00 a.m., all police officers other than Arndt had left the scene. Two BPD victims' advocates and several friends remained.

A Tragic Discovery

Sometime between 12:30 and 1:00 p.m., Arndt suggested that John and a friend search the home to see whether anything was missing. She later said she suggested this to keep John occupied. A few minutes after 1:00 p.m., John and his friend were searching the basement. In a room used for Burke's model trains, John noticed a suitcase was out of place, left beneath the basement window. John recalled breaking the window months earlier to enter the basement after getting locked out of the house.

John continued alone down a hallway through the boiler room. From there, a door led to a small storage room. The family sometimes jokingly referred to the unfinished concrete space as the "wine cellar."[8] It still contained some debris from the remodel of the home. The door had no handle, but a latch screwed into a block of wood kept it closed. When the latch was secured, the door could not be opened from the inside.

John undid the latch and entered the darkness. He turned on the light. He was met with a ghastly sight. On the dirty floor lay JonBenét. Her arms were extended above her head, and a cord was tied around each wrist. Black duct tape covered her mouth. A white blanket from her bedroom covered her torso, while her favorite pink nightgown lay on the floor next to her. John's scream was heard on the floor above.

John pulled the duct tape from his daughter's mouth and attempted to free her wrists. When he couldn't untie the knots, he picked JonBenét up, leaving the blanket behind, and carried her upstairs. She was stiff from rigor mortis and cold to the touch. John laid her on the floor of a hallway. Detective Arndt checked for a pulse. Finding none and noting the condition of the body, Arndt said, "She's dead."[9]

The detective moved JonBenét's body into the living room next to the Christmas tree. Arndt instructed John to get Patsy. After delivering the grim news, he returned to the living room and covered his daughter's body with a blanket. Moments later, Patsy entered, supported by her friends. She lay on the floor next to the body, crying and moaning as she embraced her daughter. She sobbed and prayed for a miracle. The family and their friends grew quiet as their minister said the last rites. The kidnapping case was now a murder investigation.

CHAPTER TWO

THE INVESTIGATION BEGINS

It didn't take long for the BPD to realize that it had botched the initial investigation. Its failure to secure the house after JonBenét's disappearance meant that potential evidence could have been contaminated or destroyed. BPD victims' advocates, the Ramsey family, family friends, and the Ramseys' minister were allowed to move freely throughout the home before JonBenét's body was found. Even JonBenét's body had been touched by multiple people before it was taken by police.

Panicked, the BPD scrambled to decide its next moves. At approximately 1:45 p.m., several officers returned to the home to secure the crime scene. They ordered everyone in the home to leave and sealed the doors. The Ramsey family left with only the clothes they were wearing and went to stay at the home of a friend. The BPD assigned officers as around-the-clock

Law enforcement officials would later state that the BPD's investigation was chaotic and mismanaged from the beginning.

POLICE
1737

security for the family. The officers were tasked not only with protecting the Ramseys but also with observing their behavior and conversations. Police remained with the Ramseys through December 29.

The Boulder District Attorney's (DA's) Office quickly obtained warrants to search the Ramsey house, and several officers and investigators returned to the residence at approximately 8:30 p.m. The investigators videotaped and photographed the interior and exterior of the home. Investigators searched for fingerprints and collected and tagged hundreds of items as potential evidence. They worked for ten days before unsealing the home. During those days, police also interviewed people who had been in the house that morning as well as several neighbors. The Denver and Aurora Police Departments, each with significantly more resources and homicide experience, offered to help with the investigation, but the BPD declined their offers.

Examining the Body

JonBenét's body was moved to the morgue on the evening of December 26 and stored until the autopsy the next day. The Boulder County coroner, John Meyer, supervised the transport of her body. The autopsy began at 8:15 a.m. In addition to Meyer, who performed the autopsy, two medical assistants, two attorneys from the Boulder DA's office, and two

THE CRIME SCENE

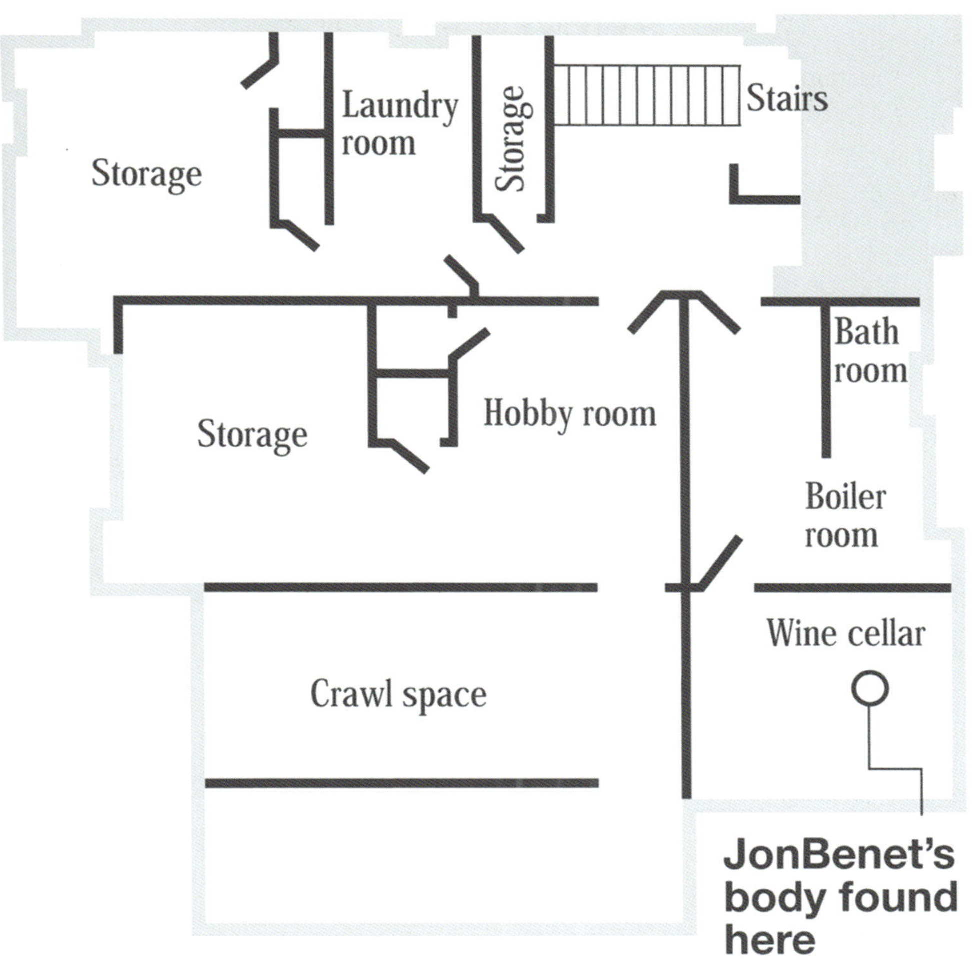

This floor plan was published in a newspaper after JonBenét's murder, showing the layout of the Ramseys' basement and the room where JonBenét's body was found.

John Meyer worked as the Boulder County coroner from 1987 to 2003.

BPD detectives attended. The exam was tape-recorded, and evidence was photographed.

Meyer began the autopsy by removing the clothing from JonBenét's body. The clothes were taken into evidence. Small spots of blood were noted on her underwear, and urine stains were found on both her underwear and long johns. Meyer also trimmed fingernails from both of JonBenét's hands to be tested later for potential sources of DNA and collected hair, eyelash, and eyebrow samples that were entered into evidence.

An examination of her skin showed abrasions on several parts of her body, indicating a struggle. Of particular note were two sets of small, roughly circular pairs of reddish marks spaced about 1.4 inches (3.6 cm) apart.[1] One set was found

on her cheek near her right ear while the other was located on
her lower back. Later investigators would wonder whether the
marks could have been made by a stun gun.

A 15.5-inch (39.4 cm) piece of white nylon cord loosely
circled JonBenét's right wrist.[2] At the other end of this cord was
another loop which her father had removed from JonBenét's
left wrist. A similar piece of cord was embedded in her neck.
That cord was knotted around a broken stick to create a garrote,
a device designed for torture. The killer likely used the weapon
to strangle the girl from behind.

The stick from the garrote was later determined to be a
piece of a paintbrush. Police found another splintered piece
of the paintbrush in the
Ramseys' basement,
near where the body
had been discovered. A
second abrasion circling
JonBenét's neck suggested
she had been strangled
twice. Small abrasions
near the cord suggested
she had clawed at the
cord with her fingernails.
Small, red marks caused
by the bursting of tiny

STUN GUNS

Stun guns are devices that deliver a
strong electric shock when their two
metal probes make contact with a
person's skin. The shock causes the
target's muscles to contract, leaving
them unable to move for several seconds.
Generally, the person will remain
conscious. Tasers are like stun guns but
can be used from a distance. Their metal
probes are attached to flexible wires that
can be launched up to 35 feet (11 m) by
compressed gas.[3]

blood vessels were noted in her eyes. These can be caused
by asphyxiation.

An examination of the victim's genital area showed a
recent wound, made just before the time of death. A few wood
fibers from the area matched the paintbrush that had been
used to fashion the garrote. Meyer believed a small area of
inflammation in another location on her genitals was caused
before the crime. He could not say conclusively whether that
injury was the result of sexual abuse or another cause, such as
an infection or wiping incorrectly after using the bathroom.

Hoping for more clarity, Meyer called a specialist from
Children's Hospital in Denver, who examined the body later that
day. That doctor could conclude only that the inflammation
might have been from prior sexual contact. Later, other
specialists reviewed the autopsy report and photographs. The
consensus of their opinions was that JonBenét had likely been
subjected to sexual contact, but not rape, prior to her time
of death.

Internal Examination of the Body

As part of the internal exam, the contents of JonBenét's
intestines were collected. Meyer described the contents as
"vegetable or fruit material which may represent fragments
of pineapple."[4] This material came from the last foods

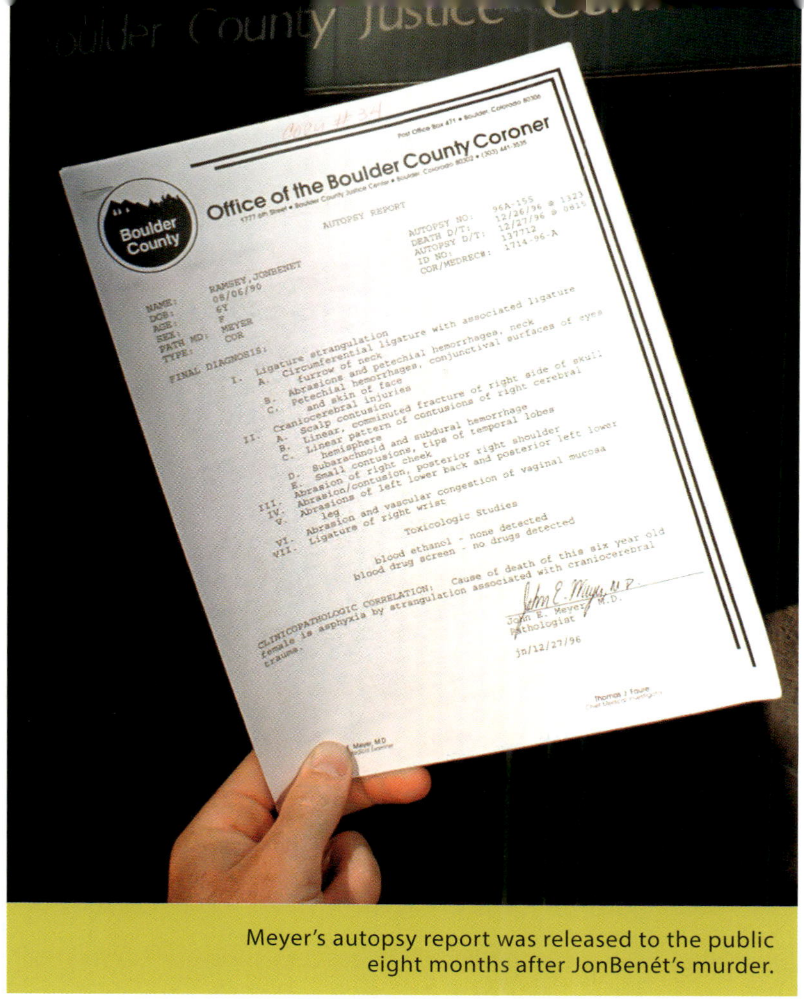

Meyer's autopsy report was released to the public eight months after JonBenét's murder.

JonBenét ate. About ten months later, the material was submitted for further testing. Two months after that, the lab reported the material contained pineapple, grapes, and cherries. Patsy said she was not aware of JonBenét eating any of those fruits on Christmas Day.

The most surprising findings came from the coroner's examination of JonBenét's skull and brain. A fracture more than eight inches (20 cm) long was found on the right side of JonBenét's skull. The blow that caused it was forceful enough to break off a piece of skull measuring about 1.75 by 0.5 inches (4.4 by 1.3 cm).[5] JonBenét had bled internally, indicating she was still alive when the injury occurred. Investigators found that the fracture had caused significant brain damage. The skin of the scalp had remained intact, so no bleeding was visible before the autopsy. Other signs of trauma would have been covered by the girl's hair.

Meyer listed JonBenét's official cause of death as "asphyxia by strangulation associated with craniocerebral trauma."[6] In his opinion, both the strangulation and the brutal blow to the head contributed to her death. He was unable to say which injury happened first. If the abrasions around her neck were caused by her clawing at the cord used to strangle her, she must have been alive and conscious during that assault. However, the bleeding associated with the skull fracture showed she was still alive when that injury occurred. Meyer later said, "I didn't know which happened first and listed them together as that's the most accurate."[7] Later, another medical examiner who reviewed Meyer's findings suggested JonBenét had been strangled twice. The examiner posited that JonBenét had been strangled once without causing death and then had received a blow to the head before being fatally strangled.

Meyer did not include an estimated time of death in his report. Police already knew that JonBenét must have been murdered sometime between 10:00 p.m., when she was put to bed, and 6:00 a.m., when police arrived at the scene. Later expert opinions did little to narrow that window.

The Ransom Note

Perhaps even more confusing than the autopsy results was the ransom note. At 372 words, the strangely lengthy note was handwritten in block letters across two and a half pages. Addressed to "Mr. Ramsey," it purported to be from a "foreign faction." Peppered with misspellings and errors, the note demanded a ransom of $118,000 and threatened to kill JonBenét if the demand was not met or the authorities were alerted. It warned that the family was being watched to ensure their compliance. The signature read "Victory! S.B.T.C."[8]

Even the existence of the note was puzzling. The killer knew that JonBenét was dead and that her body was in the house. Why pretend she was still alive and demand a ransom?

THE LINDBERGH CASE

Perhaps the most famous ransom case in American history is the March 1932 kidnapping of 20-month-old Charles Lindbergh Jr., the son of famous pilot Charles Lindbergh. A 58-word ransom note demanded $50,000 in exchange for the boy's safe return.[9] The Lindberghs paid the ransom in April, but the child's body was found in May. After the case, federal law gave the Federal Bureau of Investigation (FBI) jurisdiction in child kidnappings. The FBI responded when JonBenét was reported missing. After her body was found, the FBI removed itself from the case because local police have jurisdiction over homicides.

Whatever its intent, the note helped delay the discovery of the body by many hours—hours that led to mistakes in the investigation.

The source of the paper used for the note was determined quickly. The morning of December 26, before the discovery of JonBenét's body, John had provided handwriting samples. Not wanting to disturb his wife, he simply gave the police a pad he found in the kitchen that contained a few notes previously written by Patsy.

At about the same time the body was found, a detective with the BPD made his own discovery. The ransom note had been written on the same pad of paper John had provided. The tear marks along the top of the note matched those from three sheets on the pad. The ink from the note was later found to match a marker found in a kitchen drawer. The only fingerprints on the note belonged to an investigator. All the fingerprints found on the notepad belonged to Patsy and the police officers who had handled the items.

Additionally, police found the words "Mr. and Mrs.," followed by a vertical line, in the same block writing on another page of the notepad. The vertical line was presumed to be the downstroke of an *R* for Ramsey. It seemed the perpetrator had started a practice note. Several pages torn from the middle of the pad were never found. Either the note was written inside the Ramsey home the night of the murder or the perpetrator had previously taken the marker and notepad from the home and then returned them to the scene.

Both the family and police thought the amount of the ransom demand, $118,000, was odd. One friend remarked that the Ramseys could have afforded more than ten times that amount. John told police the amount of his Christmas bonus was $118,117.50.[10] In addition, an Access Graphics employee had previously been fired for embezzlement. The stolen amount

By May of 1997, Patsy Ramsey had given police five handwriting samples.

was very close to $118,000. Investigators also noted a Bible in the home was opened to Psalm 118.

Some of the wording of the note was unusual, including phrases such as "and, hence," "attaché case," and "fat cat." The writer switched between singular pronouns, such as "I," and plural pronouns, such as "we." The writer also alternated between addressing John Ramsey as "Mr. Ramsey" and "John." The note also referred to John as a southerner, but he wasn't from the South.[11]

Additionally, some investigators believed phrases in the note had been adapted from several popular films about murders and kidnappings. The movies investigators believed were referenced included *Dirty Harry*, *Ruthless People*, *Speed*, *Nick of Time*, and *Ransom*. For example, the villain in *Speed* says to another character, "Do not attempt to grow a brain." The ransom note says, "Don't try to grow a brain, John." These references suggested to some investigators that the crime was premeditated.[13]

The meaning of the signature, "Victory! S.B.T.C.," remains a complete mystery. Police found the use of these initials by organizations such as the Southern Bell Telephone Company and the Santa Barbara Tennis Club, but no connections between the organizations and the crime were ever identified.

At least five professional handwriting analysts compared the writing from the note with samples taken from dozens of people. All agreed that John Ramsey, Burke Ramsey, and JonBenét's half siblings could not have written the ransom note. However, when it came to Patsy, their opinions differed. One analyst with the Colorado Bureau of Investigation concluded that the evidence suggested Patsy was the author but said "the evidence falls short of that necessary to support a definite conclusion." However, an expert with the Secret Service stated there was "no evidence to indicate that Patsy Ramsey executed . . . the ransom note."[14]

The Secret Service maintains an extensive database of ink samples and determined the ink from the ransom note came from a pre-1992, black, water-based Sharpie marker.

CHAPTER THREE

THE CRIME SCENE

The size of the Ramseys' home made processing the crime scene challenging—and gave a clue about the perpetrator. They would have had to move through three levels of the large home, navigating a complicated floor plan, without being detected. Investigators concluded that the murderer knew the home well, either from spending time there or from studying the floor plans.

Unfortunately, more than 1,000 people had been in the home in the previous two years.[1] Family and friends knew the house well, as did a number of strangers. The home was part of a public holiday tour in 1994, and the Ramseys had hosted dozens of guests at holiday parties. In addition, numerous contractors had worked on the home or been given access to floor plans and blueprints during its renovation.

Police records show that a 911 call was made from the Ramsey house on December 23, just two days before JonBenét's murder. The caller hung up the phone as soon as the dispatcher answered.

Someone could even have searched the home while the Ramseys were away. The family's frequent trips left the home empty, often for weeks at a time, and though the house was equipped with an alarm system, the Ramseys didn't use it.

Possible Points of Entry

The second officer on the scene, Reichenbach, inspected the outside of the property soon after arriving on December 26. He noted no footprints in the snow or frost to indicate anyone had entered or exited the home during the night. However, he later amended his observations, explaining that the sidewalks and patio on the south side of the house and the driveway on the west side were clear of snow and frost.

Upon examining the house, investigators concluded that the perpetrator left no sign of forced entry. No windows or doors were newly broken or tampered with. However, multiple windows and exterior doors were unlocked. One of the doors

One investigator entered the Ramseys' basement through the broken window to prove it could have been a possible point of entry.

was partially open when a family friend arrived a few minutes after 6:00 a.m. on December 26. Additionally, the basement window that John had previously broken could have allowed an intruder to enter the home. This window was the focus of much attention during the investigation. No footprints were visible in the photos of the window well.

In addition, video of the window taken by investigators showed an intact spiderweb near the center of the window well outside the house, indicating no one had been in the window well. However, as many as 24 hours could have elapsed between the time an intruder entered the house and when the video was recorded, possibly leaving time for a new web to be made.

Other evidence pointed to someone using the window as an entrance. Officers observed a disturbed spiderweb in the window. In addition, a suitcase was positioned under the window, a detail John had noticed during the initial search for JonBenét. It was possible it had been used as a step to escape the house. Inside the suitcase was a pillow sham, a duvet, and a Dr. Seuss book, all belonging to JonBenét. No one in the family had packed the suitcase.

Outside, a grate over the window well showed signs of having been recently moved. Fragments from dead leaves and packing peanuts from the window well were found below the window inside the basement. This debris was also on top of the suitcase. A scuff mark ran vertically along the wall above the suitcase and below the window.

However, there were other ways an intruder could have entered the house. The Ramseys' spare key, normally hidden in front of their house, had gone missing. In addition, they had given keys to the home to family members, a housekeeper, and, during the renovation, several contractors. Many of the keys were never accounted for. Anyone with a key, or close to someone who had a key, could have easily entered the home.

Evidence inside the Home

Findings from inside the house were also difficult to interpret. There was no evidence of a struggle, though the autopsy indicated JonBenét had likely resisted her attacker. Her bedroom was in good order, and nothing seemed to be missing. Some leaf debris and packing peanuts were present in the storage room where her body was found, as was an impression from a Hi-Tec–brand work boot left in some mold and dust.

Police found other partial footprints in the storage room and on the cover of the toilet tank in the basement bathroom that did not match the Hi-Tec boot. Police also found a brown paper bag containing a rope under a bed in the bedroom next to JonBenét's. Fragments from the bag were discovered in JonBenét's bed and in the coroner's bag that had been used to store her body.

Other odd findings included a beaver hair attached to the duct tape that covered JonBenét's mouth, a body hair on the white blanket that covered her body, and brown cotton fibers on the body, the paintbrush handle, and the duct tape. The duct tape and paintbrush yielded no fingerprints or DNA.

Other fibers found on the duct tape potentially matched the jacket Patsy had worn on Christmas Day.

Another confusing piece of potential evidence was a bowl of pineapple in the Ramseys' kitchen. Investigators speculated it could have been the source of the fragments found in JonBenét's intestines, but the bowl contained no grapes or cherries, the other foods recovered during the autopsy. Also strange was that Patsy and Burke had both left fingerprints on the bowl, but JonBenét had not.

After the discovery of JonBenét's skull fracture, police hoped to find the weapon responsible at the scene. Because the blow had not broken the skin, they looked for blunt objects, such as a bat or a pipe. Investigators located a bat in the yard and identified fibers stuck to it as belonging to a carpet in the Ramseys' basement. The Ramseys reported that the bat did not belong to the family. Police also found a large police-style flashlight lying on a kitchen counter. Though the items seemed

FREQUENT DOCTOR VISITS

Soon after JonBenét's death, her medical records were leaked to the public. When people learned that JonBenét had more than 30 doctor calls and visits in the past three years, many attributed her frequent injuries and illnesses to abuse. However, Dr. Francisco Beuf, JonBenét's physician, told police that he had seen "absolutely no evidence of abuse of any kind."[2] Patsy told police that her own health scares had made her overprotective, leading her to take JonBenét to the doctor more often than necessary. Records showed that the majority of the doctor calls and visits were regarding cold and flu symptoms.

Police collected more than 1,500 pieces of evidence throughout their investigation.

to be promising candidates for the murder weapon, neither item yielded any fingerprints or DNA.

Items that were not found were also significant to the case. Police never found the remainder of the roll of duct tape used to cover JonBenét's mouth or the nylon cord used to make the garrote and bind the girl's hands. Part of the paintbrush used in the garrote was never located. Neither were several pages missing from the notepad used to write the ransom note.

Police questioned many of the Ramseys' neighbors, but they received little helpful information. One neighbor said she'd heard a child's scream between midnight and 2:00 a.m., but she later said she couldn't be certain of the date she had heard it. Another neighbor reported seeing an unfamiliar blue van near the home on December 24 and 25 but didn't have enough information to identify it. A third neighbor reported observing a dim light in the Ramseys' kitchen around midnight on the night of the crime.

CHAPTER FOUR

INVESTIGATING THE RAMSEY FAMILY

Police knew that strangers are rarely the perpetrators in child murders. Soon after the murder, JonBenét's parents became the primary suspects in the investigation. Police dove into the family's past to look for any signs that pointed toward John and Patsy's guilt.

John and Patsy Ramsey

John Bennet Ramsey was born in 1943 and grew up in Nebraska and Michigan. After graduating from high school, he attended Michigan State University, where he met his first wife, Lucinda Pasch. After college, he joined the US Navy. He was stationed in the Philippines and Atlanta, Georgia. Despite John's busy job, he and Lucinda started a family. They would eventually have three children: Beth, Melinda, and John Andrew. After leaving

John Ramsey proposed to Patsy in a restaurant in Atlanta. She waited three days to accept his proposal.

the navy, John returned to Michigan State to earn a master's degree in business administration. The family moved back to Atlanta after the completion of his degree. After 11 years of marriage, John and Lucinda's relationship ended in divorce in 1978.[1]

In the spring of 1979, John met Patricia "Patsy" Paugh. Born in West Virginia in 1956, Patsy graduated with a degree in journalism from West Virginia University. After graduation, the former Miss West Virginia 1977 moved to Atlanta for a job with an advertising agency. It was in Atlanta that Patsy would meet her future husband. Patsy and John were introduced to one another at a dinner party. After two years of dating, the couple married in November 1980.

After moving to an Atlanta suburb, the Ramseys started a computer software company out of their home. The company grew, and in the late 1980s it merged with two other companies to become Access Graphics. The Ramsey family also grew with the birth

ACCESS GRAPHICS

In the late 1980s, the aerospace company Lockheed bought a 25 percent interest in John Ramsey's growing business, Access Graphics.[2] In 1995, Lockheed merged with Martin Marietta. Soon after, the new corporation, Lockheed Martin, bought the remainder of Access Graphics. John stayed as chief executive officer. The business also had offices in Mexico and the Netherlands. General Electric bought the company in 1997 and fired John later that year.

of Burke in January 1987 and JonBenét in August 1990. In 1991, the Ramseys moved to Boulder to be near the Access Graphics headquarters.

Though no longer living in the same household, John remained close to his children from his previous marriage. In 1996, John Andrew was a student at the University of Colorado and spent many of his weekends and school breaks with his father and stepmother, of whom he was fond. That year, he spent Christmas with his mother and Melinda in Atlanta.

Victims or Killers?

Only three people were known to be with JonBenét the night of her death: her father, mother, and brother. Police quickly homed in on the parents as their top suspects. The absence of any signs of struggle inside the home suggested the killer was known to JonBenét. The lack of evidence of forced entry cast doubt on the idea that an intruder had invaded the home.

FILICIDE IN THE UNITED STATES

Compared with other countries, the United States has a high rate of child murders. The most common perpetrator of these crimes is a child's own parent. Murder of one's child is called filicide. About 500 filicides are committed in the United States every year.[4] Common factors in filicide include poverty, a previous history of physical abuse by the parent, young parental age, parental substance abuse, and single or divorced parents.

When the autopsy results suggested previous sexual abuse, scrutiny focused on John. Some investigators theorized that he had been molesting his daughter and killed her to hide it.

However, that theory started to unravel quickly. Police contacted current and former teachers, friends, and doctors of John's children. No one had ever suspected abuse. His ex-wife defended him as well, saying, "John would never murder his child."[3] Investigators found John had no history of violence, substance abuse, or pornography use, risk factors for parental abuse of a child. In addition, multiple expert handwriting analysts all agreed he could not have written the ransom note.

Soon, attention shifted to Patsy Ramsey. Boulder Police detective Steve Thomas developed a theory that Patsy had become angry at JonBenét for wetting her bed. He hypothesized that Patsy had struck or pushed JonBenét, causing the young girl's head trauma. Then, suspecting the injury would be fatal, she strangled and sexually assaulted her daughter, staging the crime scene and ransom note to cover up the crime.

Pieces of the evidence fit the theory well. Some experts believed Patsy could have written the ransom note, and the notepad and marker belonged to her. The paintbrush used to make the garrote belonged to Patsy as well. Analysts thought the body hair on the white blanket could have come from Patsy, and fibers from her jacket matched fibers found on the duct tape that covered JonBenét's mouth. Patsy was also observed wearing the same sweater on both December 25 and 26, suggesting to some that she had never gone to sleep, possibly because she spent the night killing her daughter and staging the crime scene.

Additionally, investigators wondered why the Ramseys would have called the police so quickly after finding the ransom note. After all, the ransom note threatened to kill JonBenét if the Ramseys alerted the police. Patsy defended herself against this remark, stating that calling the police was an instinctive reaction, and in her panic, she had read only the first few lines of the note. Skeptics of that explanation point out that Patsy was able to relate the signature to the 911 dispatcher. Patsy said John had spread the pages

JonBenét's name came from combining her father's first and middle names: John Bennet.

of the note on the floor and she was able to read the note over his shoulder.

Other evidence seemed to rule out Patsy as the culprit. The autopsy found signs that JonBenét had struggled against the garrote, but medical experts agreed that if the blow to the head had come first, she would not have been conscious when she was strangled. In addition, although JonBenét's clothes were urine stained, her sheets were not. Thomas suggested Patsy could have changed the sheets, but analysis proved this unlikely. The sheets on the bed contained fibers from the clothing JonBenét was wearing when she died, fibers that wouldn't have been present if the sheets had been washed.

Several movie references are made throughout the ransom note. Supporters of John and Patsy pointed out that the couple didn't watch movies.

Patsy also did not fit the profile of someone who would kill a child. Like John, she had no history of violence or substance abuse, and everyone who knew the family said she was a gentle and doting mother. Family and friends doubted bed-wetting or any other behavior could have elicited such a violent reaction.

Other skeptics of this theory have pointed out the improbability of Patsy creating such an elaborate cover story. Some argue that if Patsy had struck out in a moment of rage, she would have been more likely to call an ambulance than stage such a complex and horrific crime scene. It seemed unlikely that she would instead write a strange ransom note, commit a sexual assault, inflict two matching sets of odd circular wounds on her daughter, and stage the basement to suggest someone had entered through the window. In addition, they point out that despite extensive searches, the remainder of the duct tape and cord used during the murder were never found in the home.

Some supporters of this theory suggest that Patsy had help. Some theorize that John woke up at some point during the night, discovered his wife's actions, and, realizing it was too late to save JonBenét, covered for Patsy. Critics of this idea suggest that if John had participated in the cover-up, he would not have given the notepad used for the ransom note to the police or allowed himself to be the one to discover the body. At least one investigator speculated that on the morning of December 26,

John was ignorant of his wife's actions, but that some time later Patsy confessed or John surmised the facts of the crime and then became part of the deception.

The Brothers as Suspects

Other members of the public suspected Burke was responsible for the murder. These theories were bolstered when tabloids falsely reported that he had been named a suspect. Several scenarios were invented to explain the crime. Some people theorized that late on Christmas night, JonBenét angered her brother, and the nine-year-old struck her forcefully enough to cause a skull fracture. These theorists posited that Burke then reported the injury to Patsy, and, guessing the injury was fatal, Patsy strangled her daughter to protect her son. Under Colorado law, a nine-year-old could not have been criminally charged, but Patsy might have been unaware of that.

Burke Ramsey recalled his sister's funeral being traumatizing.

Alternatively, Patsy might have feared she would lose custody of her son. John might have assisted Patsy or discovered the truth after the fact.

Supporters of this theory claim that Burke had a history of violence. The Ramseys had reported in August 1994 that Burke accidentally struck his sister with a golf club. Some believe that

Though some theorize that Burke Ramsey, *right*, was jealous of the attention JonBenét, *left*, was given, Burke said his parents treated the siblings equally.

the incident wasn't an accident and that Burke had previously become angry enough to attack his sister. Some even suspect that Burke could have been sexually assaulting his sister.

Skeptics point out that Burke's teachers and family reported no history of violence or concerns about his behavior. In addition, Burke was interviewed by a detective without his parents present soon after the discovery of his sister's body on December 26. No one had informed him of his sister's death,

Alex Hunter served as the Boulder district attorney from 1973 to 2001.

and he seemed unaware that she had died. The detective did not note anything suspicious in the interview. Burke was interviewed again by a child psychologist from the Boulder County Department of Social Services 13 days after the murder, also without his parents present.

The psychologist described Burke as small for his age and shy but bright. She noted that he did not have any specific knowledge of his sister's murder and concluded that Burke "was not a witness to JonBenét's death."[5] For Burke to have been the killer, the nine-year-old boy would have had to successfully deceive both a trained detective and a child psychologist. In response to reports naming Burke as the culprit, District Attorney Alex Hunter issued a statement that Burke was not a suspect.

Others named John Andrew, JonBenét's half brother, as the killer. Police quickly confirmed that he had been in Atlanta with his sister and mother the night of the homicide. However, conspiracy theories about how he could have committed the murder continued to circulate online for years.

John Andrew Ramsey has joined his father's efforts to find JonBenét's killer by pushing for further investigation and raising awareness about the crime on social media.

CHAPTER FIVE

PRESSURE BUILDS

By the evening of December 26, news of the murder had spread locally. The next morning, a Colorado newspaper called the *Daily Camera* ran its first story about the crime. The article reported that police said they had no suspects. Privately, however, police had already begun to suspect JonBenét's parents.

On the evening of December 27, Detective Arndt and another detective visited the Ramseys, hoping to question them or schedule further interviews. The Ramseys were staying at the home of a friend. Though the police wanted to question the Ramseys at the BPD, the family's doctor said the parents were too distraught to travel. Additionally, Patsy was medicated and unable to answer questions. However, John spoke with police for about 40 minutes and offered to answer further

Within two days of her death, JonBenét's murder had attracted widespread media attention.

BOULDER P
Local news, Loca
A New Hope Group Publication
'The heart of God is broken'
— the Rev. W. Frank Harrington
Ramsey murder shocks city, nation
Brutalized body of JonBenet Ramsey, 6, buried in Atlanta; Boulder beauty queen was found gagged, strangled
"There is nothing standard about this case."
— Tom Koby, Boulder police chief
INSIDE:
Killer used cord
strangle Ramsey,
gagged her wit
and, so
JonBen
Quickly
See page 6
See Sports, Page 16

questions at the home where the family was staying. The police declined.

Later that evening, John received a call from a friend letting him know that he had been contacted by someone working in the Boulder DA's office. The employee had said that the police were targeting the Ramseys. John's friend advised John to hire attorneys for himself and Patsy. However, John was too grief-stricken to search for lawyers. On December 28, John's friend hired attorneys for the Ramseys.

On the afternoon of December 28, the Ramsey family reported to the Boulder Sheriff's Department and provided samples of handwriting, DNA, blood, fingerprints, and hair. The BPD requested the family report to the department for more questioning. The family declined but repeated their offer to talk to investigators at the home where they were staying. However, police refused to conduct the questioning outside their office.

THE FOLLOWING DAYS

Though information leaked to the media described the Ramseys as acting removed and uncaring in the days following JonBenét's murder, the BPD officer who remained with the family reported the parents were shocked, hysterical, and distraught. The officer's report from the first night after the murder detailed the parents' state. His notes described the parents collapsing on the living room floor, sobbing, pacing, and repeatedly checking on Burke's safety. Even still, Hunter referred to John as "ice man" after delivering unsubstantiated reports of the father's cold demeanor.[1]

JonBenét Ramsey was buried in St. James Episcopal
Church Cemetery in Marietta, Georgia.

They threatened to hold JonBenét's body until the Ramseys
agreed to questioning at the BPD. An attorney representing the
Ramseys asked the DA and coroner's offices to intervene. The
offices informed the BPD that they had no legal authority to
hold the young girl's body. That event was the beginning of
tensions between the BPD and the DA's office that would linger
for years and hinder the investigation.

December 29 was Patsy's fortieth birthday. Instead of a
party, she attended a memorial service for her daughter at
the family's church in Boulder. Afterward, the Ramseys flew to
Georgia for JonBenét's funeral. The family considered Atlanta,
the city where JonBenét had been born, their hometown. A
visitation at a funeral home was held on December 30, followed
by a funeral at Peachtree Presbyterian Church the next day.

Publicity Grows

By the day of the funeral, false reports began appearing in media outlets, including claims that Patsy had refused to give DNA samples and that the family had refused all police interviews. Meanwhile, JonBenét's image was appearing in media nationwide. Much of the coverage focused on JonBenét's participation in beauty pageants. Hilary Levey Friedman, a Harvard sociologist who studied pageants, later said the "combination of wealth, attractiveness, the mystery of the murder and then the child beauty pageant angle made [the murder] a national and international story."[2]

Media outlets bought pageant images and videos from pageant photographers. Since the Ramseys hadn't taken the photos, they didn't own the images and had no say in how they were used. Generally, the public judged the pageants to be exploitative. Many people viewed the Ramseys as bad parents for encouraging JonBenét's participation in the child beauty pageants.

Cable news channel CNN contacted the Ramseys and offered them a chance to appear on national television on January 1, 1997. John later said that he and Patsy thought the interview would allow them to appeal to a larger audience for help in finding their daughter's killer. However, the interview's most immediate consequence was to amplify media scrutiny of both the investigation and the Ramsey family.

DNA Evidence

Many investigators hoped that DNA testing would be the key to solving the murder, but in the end, it raised more questions than answers. JonBenét's fingernail clippings yielded very small amounts of unidentified DNA. In January 1997, testing revealed it was a mixed sample containing material from two males and one female. The strongest sample in the mix came from a male. None of the DNA matched any of JonBenét's family members. Police thought the clippers used by the coroner may have contaminated the sample. They obtained and tested DNA from the eight autopsies prior to JonBenét's. None matched. Due to the poor quality of the samples, the results were not robust enough to be compared with databases of known and suspected criminals' DNA.

Patsy Ramsey was on antianxiety medication and tranquilizers during her interview with CNN. The medication made her seem disoriented and confused, which many interpreted as signs of guilt.

A third sample of DNA was obtained from a bloodstain in JonBenét's underwear. The blood belonged to JonBenét, but mixed with the blood was enough unidentified DNA to produce a sample. It matched the DNA profile from the strongest sample obtained from JonBenét's fingernail clippings. Investigators dubbed the person the sample belonged to as Unknown Male #1. Unfortunately, it also was not suitable for comparison with databases.

The BPD withheld these first DNA test results from the media and the Boulder DA's office. This would later worsen the tense relationship between the BPD and the DA. The BPD explained that it was afraid the DA's office might leak the information. Critics pointed out that the BPD was willing to leak information that incriminated the family but not information that supported their innocence.

The Investigation Stalls

Over the next several months, investigators interviewed nearly 400 people and collected 63 handwriting samples and 45 DNA samples, but no significant progress was made in the case.[3] In spite of this, national and even international media coverage continued. The relationships among the Ramsey family, the BPD, and the Boulder DA's office deteriorated amid allegations of deceit and media manipulation. At one point, the BPD agreed to question John and Patsy at a location outside of its offices. Briefly, it seemed cooperation between the police and the family might be improving, but the BPD canceled those interviews at the last minute.

JonBenét's funeral was held in the same church that hosted her parents' wedding and her own christening.

On April 18, 1997, Hunter officially named John and Patsy Ramsey as "the focus of the investigation."[4] If, as some commentators suggested, the move was calculated to put pressure on the Ramseys, it worked, at least to a degree. John and Patsy both consented to interrogations that took place on April 30.

Some details from the Ramseys' interrogations conflicted with one another or with information in the police reports about interviews conducted from December 26 to 28.

After repeated missteps, Detective Linda Arndt, *left*, was removed from JonBenét Ramsey's case in May 1997.

For example, John and Patsy gave slightly different estimates of the time the family left the Christmas party the night before JonBenét's murder. In addition, Patsy had said in an earlier interview that she had looked into JonBenét's room before finding the ransom note, but she denied that in the April interrogations. These inconsistencies could indicate deliberate deception, confusion caused by the traumatic event, or faded memories in the months between the crime and the interrogations.

Additionally, some of the discrepancies might have been the result of police errors. Because the early interviews weren't recorded, details were impossible to verify. Standard police procedure required Arndt, the only officer on the scene when JonBenét's body was discovered, to file her report about the day within 48 hours. However, Arndt didn't file her report until 13 days later, when her memory would have been less clear and possibly influenced by subsequent events and media coverage. Even the arrival times officers listed in their reports conflicted with notes taken at the scene on December 26. If they had made errors about such straightforward facts, they might have made other mistakes.

On May 1, 1997, the day after the Ramseys' interrogations, the Ramsey family held a press conference to defend themselves against public suspicions. They also publicized their offer of a $100,000 reward for information that led to progress in the case.[5] Attendance was by invitation only, and lawyers carefully controlled the event.

As the months passed, law enforcement investigated tips, returned to the crime scene, and consulted experts about evidence. After initial missteps, the subsequent investigation was exhaustive, generating tens of thousands of pages of documents and costing nearly $2 million.[6] Still, the case ran cold.

The Grand Jury

In March 1998, the BPD requested that Hunter convene a grand jury. Grand juries work differently than traditional trials. In criminal trials, both the prosecution and the defense submit evidence and question witnesses. In grand jury proceedings, only the prosecution presents a case. No defense is made. Jurors then vote on whether the evidence is convincing enough to formally charge suspects with a crime and, if so, which crimes to charge them with. Grand juries allow prosecutors to test the strength of their arguments and evidence and create legal authority to subpoena reluctant witnesses and confidential records and documents.

Before Hunter agreed to the request, he asked the BPD to present its evidence to his office and other experts. Three months later, Hunter announced his office would call a grand jury. Some observers hailed the decision as an important step in pursuing justice for JonBenét. Others questioned why a grand jury wasn't convened earlier to aid the investigation. Still others believed the move was politically motivated. Because grand jury proceedings are secret, Hunter could appear to be proactive on the case without releasing any information that might damage public opinion of himself or his office.

Beginning on September 15, 1998, the jury met for more than a year, listening to testimony from investigators, forensics

DETECTIVE STEVE THOMAS

Steve Thomas was a detective for the BPD narcotics unit in 1996. He had no homicide experience but was assigned to investigate JonBenét's murder days after the crime. Thomas resigned from the BPD in August 1998 after the district attorney refused to let him and other BPD detectives participate in the grand jury case. In his resignation letter, he said the case "became a nearly impossible investigation because of political alliances, philosophical differences and professional egos."[7]

Hundreds of journalists surrounded Alex Hunter as he announced the outcome of the grand jury investigation.

experts, and friends and associates of the Ramseys. The family asked to be subpoenaed. John and Patsy were not called as witnesses, but Burke, John Andrew, and Melinda Ramsey all gave testimony. Also excluded were several BPD detectives who had played key roles in the investigation. Although the proceedings were secret, media stayed outside the Boulder County Justice Center to try to identify witnesses as they entered and hounded them for details and report leaks.

In October 1999, Hunter announced the grand jury had completed its investigation and stated, "We do not have sufficient evidence to warrant filing charges against anyone who has been investigated at the present time."[8] No other information about the grand jury proceedings was released for 14 years.

CHAPTER SIX

THE INTRUDER THEORY

n March 1997, the Boulder DA's office hired Lou Smit to work on the Ramsey case. Smit had decades of experience investigating homicides, including several high-profile cases. Smit came to the job with John and Patsy at the top of his list of suspects, but he soon changed his mind. Smit's examination of the evidence convinced him an intruder had murdered JonBenét. John Douglas, an FBI profiler hired by the Ramseys, supported this theory.

Smit's Intruder Theory

Smit believed the window leading to the basement had been the intruder's point of entry into the house. He pointed to the disturbed vegetation and the scuff mark on the wall below the window. He believed the suitcase was used by the intruder to

At the time he joined the Ramsey investigation, Lou Smit had 30 years of investigative experience.

JonBenet

step up to the window when exiting the home. Perhaps it was initially intended to carry JonBenét or her body. This theory was supported by forensic examinations. Fibers from the linens in the suitcase were found on the clothes JonBenét was wearing when she was killed. The contents of the suitcase and the pink nightgown found next to the body might have been intended to soothe JonBenét or be kept as trophies of the crime but were later abandoned, possibly in the effort to exit the home.

Skeptics pointed to the undisturbed spiderweb and lack of footprints in the window well to dismiss Smit's theory. However, Smit argued that the intruder could have avoided the web or that the web could have been made after the crime. He believed any footprints were likely brushed away and covered with leaf debris and packing material. Other intruder theory supporters have pointed to other possible means of entry, including another window, the rear door to the kitchen that was found slightly open, and keys given to friends and contractors.

Smit also cited the unusual sets of circular marks on
JonBenét's skin as evidence of an attack by an intruder. He
thought the injuries were made by the leads of a stun gun. An
intruder, unlike a family member, would have needed a way to
subdue the child and keep her quiet while she was removed
from her bedroom. A stun
gun, Smit said, would have
allowed the perpetrator
to quietly take the girl
without a struggle.

**Lou Smit came out of retirement
to join the Ramsey investigation.**

Smit theorized that, once in the basement, the perpetrator
placed duct tape on JonBenét's mouth, cords around her wrists,
and a garrote around her neck to help control the victim. When
JonBenét struggled, she left abrasions on her torso and neck.
Perhaps in response to her struggle, the perpetrator used the
stun gun a second time and inflicted a blow to the head. The
trauma could have caused her to lose bladder control, leaving
urine stains on her clothes.

Smit even identified the brand and model of stun gun likely
used in the crime. A closer examination of the wounds might
have allowed investigators to confirm or rule out this theory.
However, by the time Smit proposed this idea, the body had
been buried for several months and had begun to decompose.

Smit said that an intruder could have entered the house
while the Ramseys were at a dinner party Christmas night

and may have been in the house for several hours before they returned, giving the perpetrator plenty of time to write the lengthy ransom note. The intruder might have even brought notes from movie scripts to include. Smit said it was also possible the intruder had been in the home before and removed the notepad and marker. Then, on the night of the crime, the killer could have returned with the items and the completed ransom note.

Smit was unsure whether the intruder had ever intended to kidnap JonBenét or if the perpetrator had always been intent on murder. The intruder may have believed that by removing the body, he could profit from a ransom. The night of the crime, however, the intruder may have found removing the body impractical. Or, as many investigators believed, the note might always have been intended to confuse the family and police, delaying the investigation.

According to the Ramseys, learning that JonBenét tried to fight
against her murderer left them with nights and days of agony.

Former FBI profiler John Douglas was hired by the Ramseys to investigate JonBenét's murder.

Smit failed to convince most of the investigators within the BPD that an intruder killed JonBenét, but his theory gained more traction with the Boulder DA's office. Still, he resigned from the case in September 1998, feeling the investigation was too focused on the family. He wrote that he could not "in good conscience be a part of the persecution of innocent people."[4]

Who and Why?

If an intruder killed JonBenét, the list of suspects is long. Investigators such as Smit and Douglas believed the perpetrator was a pedophile. He might have noticed JonBenét in a pageant.

He might even have been stalking and grooming her. Some
theorists point toward JonBenét's mention of a promised
visit from Santa as evidence that someone was grooming her.
Others think the perpetrator was connected to John. Perhaps
he harbored anger toward John over business dealings or
believed John was flaunting his wealth. If the intruder had a
connection with John, then he likely had access to the home
and, possibly, to JonBenét before the crime.

Supporters of the intruder theory point to similar cases of
kidnappings and murders. For example, in 1991, Heather Dawn
Church was taken from
her Colorado Springs,
Colorado, home and
murdered by a man living
nearby who had been
stalking her. Initially,
her father had been the
primary suspect. In 2002,
Elizabeth Smart was
kidnapped from her home
in Salt Lake City, Utah,
and held for nine months
by a man who had done
odd jobs in her home
months earlier.

THE HEATHER DAWN CHURCH MURDER

Heather Dawn Church was 13 years old
when she went missing on September 17,
1991. A camper found her skull two years
later. Lou Smit joined the investigation in
1995 and sent fingerprints from the scene
to more than 100 identification systems.
A match led to the arrest of Robert
Charles Browne, who was sentenced to
life in prison. Browne later claimed he
killed at least 48 people, starting in the
1970s. This confession led to a second
homicide conviction.[5]

CHAPTER SEVEN

THE RAMSEY CASE IN THE MEDIA

n the mid-1990s, news outlets were in transition. The growth of cable television news programs and whole networks dedicated to news reporting created demand for breaking stories and new perspectives around the clock. The internet was also becoming a source for news. Internet news increased the pressure to find stories that could attract the public in this new 24-hour news cycle. High-profile crimes, such as JonBenét's murder, helped to fill that demand.

A Media Storm

The first reports about JonBenét's murder came from local news outlets on December 26, 1996, the same day JonBenét's body was found. By December 28, the story had been picked up by newspapers across the country. It was the beginning of what

JonBenét's murder quickly became a popular topic for tabloids, books, newspapers, documentaries, and more.

SOCIAL SECURITY: PLAYING RETIREMENT ROULETTE
Newsweek
The Strange World of JonBenet
er Life in
e Spotlight—
nd Mysterious
ath
People
MURDER OF A LITTLE BEAUTY
Heartbreak in Colorado
The brutal killing
of pageant princess
JonBenet Ramsey, 6,
shocks the nation—
and raises troubling
questions

one reporter described as "an explosion of voyeuristic interest."[1] On New Year's Eve, both NBC and CBS reported on the crime on prime-time evening newscasts, even airing pageant videos.

That day, as the Ramseys were burying their daughter, the family got a taste of the intensity of the coming media storm. Photographers and camera crews waited outside the church where the funeral was held. After being asked to leave the cemetery, the media camped out across the street to watch the burial service.

THE O. J. SIMPSON CASE

On June 12, 1994, Nicole Brown Simpson and one of her friends were found stabbed to death. Five days later, after a high-speed chase broadcast on live television, police arrested O. J. Simpson, a former football star and Brown Simpson's ex-husband. In October 1995, a jury found Simpson not guilty in a criminal trial, but in February 1997, a civil jury found him liable for wrongful death. Media coverage of the case drew viewers and readers for almost three years. As the Simpson case moved out of the spotlight, the Ramsey case became a similarly high-profile news story.

In the spring of 1997, the friend with whom the Ramseys were staying called the BPD to complain that reporters were harassing her children as they waited for their school bus. She also said reporters were knocking on their door and searching their trash. The Ramseys spent the summer of 1997 at their home in Michigan before moving back to Atlanta in the fall. Reporters and

In September 1997, the Ramseys learned that someone,
likely a tabloid reporter, installed a hidden camera
on a utility post to film JonBenét's grave.

photographers followed them wherever they went. At times,
John and Patsy thought about moving to a new country or
dying by suicide to escape the turmoil.

Some of what the media reported was false or misleading.
Often the misinformation was the result of sloppy journalistic
practices. Paula Woodward, a television journalist based in
Denver, later wrote, "In many cases, reporters failed to ensure
the accuracy of the information they were reporting due to the

immense pressure they faced to be first."[2] For example, a *Rocky Mountain News* journalist reported on January 1, 1997, that John had piloted the plane the family took to Atlanta for the funeral. In fact, Lockheed Martin, the parent company of Access Graphics, had provided both the plane and the pilots for the cross-country trip. The reporter eventually admitted he had relied on a single source for information that later proved to be wrong.

In other instances, law enforcement released misinformation. On December 31, 1996, the BPD public information officer told the press that Patsy had not provided any blood, hair, or handwriting samples even though all three had been given to the BPD by December 28. The BPD issued a press release correcting the mistake on January 2, but by that time the incriminating statement had been picked up by newspapers and was being discussed on talk shows. The BPD gave no explanation for the mistake.

The Strategic Use of Media

Some leaks were designed by police to put pressure on the Ramseys by turning public opinion against them. In February 1997, such a report was made to a local Boulder newspaper. An article in the *Daily Camera* revealed that the BPD had consulted with Marilyn Van Derbur, former Miss America 1958 and a survivor of incest, who had become an advocate for child sexual abuse survivors. The report led to extensive media speculation that the BPD had evidence that John had molested his daughter, evidence that didn't exist.

On February 13, 1997, Hunter delivered a message to the media designed to intimidate the perpetrator. He said the

After revealing the abuse she suffered from her father, Marilyn Van Derbur became an advocate for survivors of incest.

"list of suspects narrows. Soon there will be no one on the list but you."[4] He later told a journalist that the message was meant to target Patsy. However, after watching the press conference on the news, Patsy called Hunter to thank him for his work on the case.

The following day, February 14, 26-year-old Michael Helgoth was found dead of a gunshot wound in his Boulder home. Detectives found a pair of Hi-Tec boots, a stun gun, and a 9-mm pistol in his home. Helgoth's DNA was tested by the BPD but didn't match that of Unknown Male #1. The death was ruled a suicide. A private investigator hired by the Ramseys questioned that determination. He suggested Helgoth knew something about the murder and had been killed by the perpetrator, perhaps in response to Hunter's statement to the press.

The Murder Comes to Bookstores

As months became years and the case remained unsolved, media attention grew to include books and documentaries. The first of dozens of books about the case, *Perfect Murder, Perfect Town: The Uncensored Story of the JonBenét Murder and the Grand Jury's Search for the Final Truth*, was released in 1999. The date coincided with the conclusion of the grand jury proceedings and Hunter's announcement that no charges would be filed. In its more than 800 pages, crime writer Lawrence Schiller

The 2000 docudrama *Perfect Murder, Perfect Town: JonBenét and the City of Boulder* starred Dyanne Iandoli, *bottom right*, as JonBenét Ramsey.

reported on the evidence, tensions between the BPD and the Boulder DA's office, and perspectives from dozens of people associated with the case and the Ramseys. He did not endorse any specific theory about the identity of the killer. The book was the basis for a television docudrama produced in 2000.

Many later books proposed specific theories about what had happened. After resigning from the BPD in 1998, Steve Thomas wrote a book that hit store shelves in April 2000. *JonBenét: Inside the Ramsey Murder Investigation* presents

Thomas's theory. Like many in the BPD, Thomas believed Patsy had killed her daughter, likely because of bed-wetting, and John had covered for his wife. In 2001, the Ramseys sued Thomas and his publisher for libel. A year later, the case was settled out of court. The publisher paid an undisclosed amount in damages.

In 2012, A. James Kolar published *Foreign Faction: Who Really Kidnapped JonBenét?* Kolar, an investigator with the Boulder DA's office from 2004 to 2006, begins with a detailed theory naming a group of kidnappers turned killers committing the crime to exact revenge on John. By the end of the book, however, it is clear Kolar has discounted that idea and believes Burke killed his sister and one or both of his parents staged much of the evidence to protect him.

The Ramseys' attorney says that Kolar's claim that Burke killed JonBenét is nonsense.

Other books support the intruder theory. Among them are two books by journalist Paula Woodward, titled *We Have Your Daughter: The Unsolved Murder of JonBenét Ramsey Twenty Years Later* and *Unsolved: The JonBenét Ramsey Murder 25 Years Later*. Detective John Anderson's *Lou and JonBenét: A Legendary Lawman's Quest to Solve a Child Beauty Queen's Murder*, released in February 2023, was another book supporting the intruder theory. The book highlights Lou Smit's life and his dedication to solving JonBenét's murder.

Lawsuits and the Court of Public Opinion

In the absence of a real trial, there was a flurry of speculation and accusations over who was responsible for JonBenét's murder. In November 1997, the daytime talk show *Geraldo*, hosted by Geraldo Rivera, broadcast a mock trial of John and Patsy. Some of the witnesses were tabloid reporters. The jury, in a four-to-two vote, found the couple guilty.

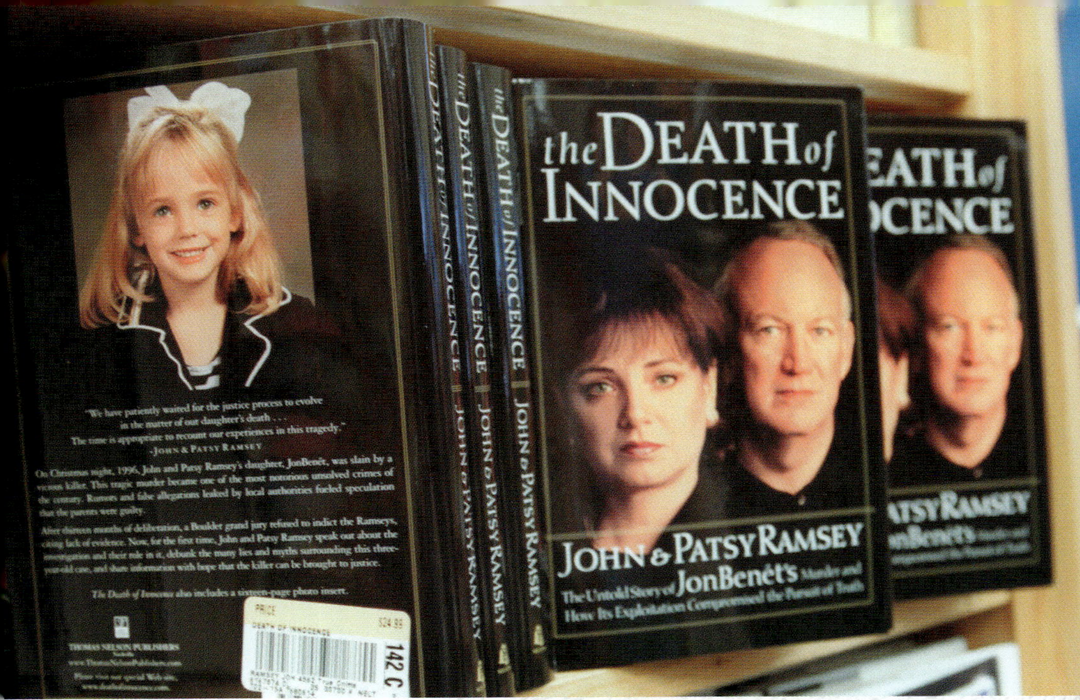

The Ramseys said that all proceeds from their memoir would go toward legal fees and a charity they founded in JonBenét's name.

The Ramseys also used the media to make their case to the public. They gave interviews in January and May 1997. In March 2000, they talked to journalist Barbara Walters on *20/20*. John had a second interview with her in 2015. John and Patsy also coauthored their own book, *The Death of Innocence: The Untold Story of JonBenét's Murder and How Its Exploitation Compromised the Pursuit of Truth*, which was released in 2000. Critics accused them of trying to profit from their daughter's murder. The Ramseys replied that they were trying to defend themselves against false accusations and persuade the police to investigate other suspects.

One of the suspects mentioned in the Ramseys' book was Robert Christian Wolf, whose ex-girlfriend reported him to police, saying he had disappeared Christmas night and had been behaving suspiciously. Wolf sued the Ramseys for their accusations, arguing that he was falsely accused by the family. A key point in the lawsuit was whether the Ramseys were themselves guilty of the murder. If they were, identifying others as suspects could constitute defamation. If they weren't, presenting Wolf as a suspect would have been a reasonable action for the family of a victim.

Wolf's case never went to trial. Julie E. Carnes, the judge assigned to the case, issued her decision based on evidence given in depositions by the family, investigators, and other witnesses. She dismissed the case with a 93-page ruling that concluded, "The weight of the evidence is more consistent with a theory that an intruder murdered JonBenét than it is with a theory that Mrs. Ramsey did so."[6] The ruling

After claiming she had a vision of JonBenét's killer, professed psychic Dorothy Allison created a sketch of the alleged suspect. The Ramseys posted the sketch on their website in 2000.

criticized the mistakes made by the BPD and the role of the media in the case. Carnes further affirmed that the Ramseys had cooperated with police and discredited the theory that John had been complicit in any cover-up.

The Death of Innocence led to another lawsuit, this time brought against the Ramseys by Linda Hoffmann-Pugh, their

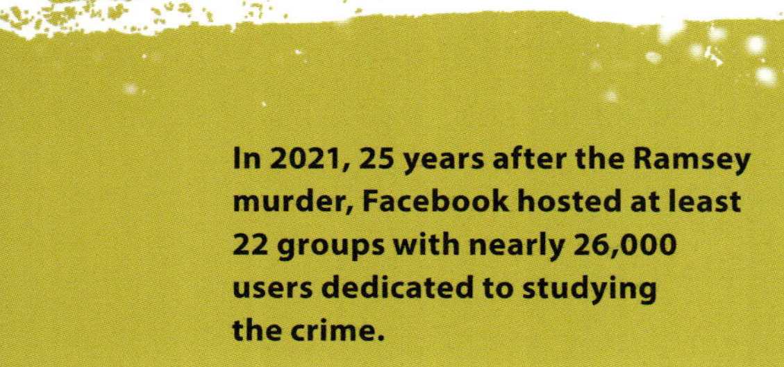

In 2021, 25 years after the Ramsey murder, Facebook hosted at least 22 groups with nearly 26,000 users dedicated to studying the crime.

former housekeeper. She alleged the book presented her falsely as a suspect. This case was settled with the Ramseys paying no damages.

Despite lawsuit rulings in favor of the Ramseys, public suspicions lingered on the family. These suspicions were bolstered on October 23, 2013, when a judge ordered the release of two indictments recommended by the 1999 grand jury. The jury had voted in favor of charging both John and Patsy with two crimes. The first was "permit[ting] a child to be unreasonably placed in a situation which posed a threat of injury to the child's life or health." The second was "render[ing] assistance to a person . . . knowing the person being assisted has committed and was suspected of the crime of murder in the first degree."[7]

The text of the two recommended charges bolstered theories that John and Patsy Ramsey had been involved in JonBenét's death. However, this was speculation, as none of the transcripts of the grand jury proceedings were released and the jurors remained under an oath of secrecy.

Suspicions also lingered on JonBenét's brother, with books such as Kolar's feeding into the public's theories. In 2016, CBS added fuel to the suspicions when the company released a

Burke, *right*, said that the last time he saw his sister, *left*, alive was in the car on the way back from the Christmas party.

During his interview, Burke said that he believes a pedophile murdered JonBenét after seeing her in a beauty pageant.

documentary titled *The Case of: JonBenét Ramsey*, produced for the twentieth anniversary of the murder. The four-hour miniseries relied heavily on Kolar's book and presented opinions from experts, some involved in the case and some not, who believe Burke killed his sister.

John and Burke sued CBS and Kolar for defamation over the documentary's claims. The case was settled when CBS agreed to pay damages, but the amount was not made public. Over the years, the Ramseys filed a total of nine lawsuits against various media outlets. Eight were decided in the Ramseys' favor. In the case decided against them, no damages were awarded.

Since his sister's death, Burke has consistently avoided media attention with one notable exception. Knowing *The Case of: JonBenét Ramsey* was about to air, he made an appearance on the *Dr. Phil* talk show in September 2016. Besides recounting what he remembered about the event and denying any involvement, Burke gave his reason for staying out of the spotlight. He told host Phil McGraw, "I wanted to grow up like a normal kid."[8]

In the years since the murder, the growth of the internet has allowed anyone interested in the crime to participate in chats or produce websites, podcasts, and YouTube videos about JonBenét's death. A quick search will find hundreds of these forums and productions. Often the credentials and even identities of the people responsible for this content are unknown. This has led to the spread of misinformation and conspiracy theories about the case. One of the strangest, which surfaced on the internet in 2014, claimed JonBenét didn't die; after her murder was staged, she assumed another identity and grew up to become pop star Katy Perry.

The case has been so highly publicized that few associated with it have escaped media scrutiny. The family, other suspects, individual investigators, the BPD, and the Boulder DA's office have all been put on trial in the court of public opinion. Despite the whirlwind of allegations, no one has been convicted of JonBenét's murder.

CHAPTER EIGHT

DEAD ENDS AND LINGERING HOPE

The extensive media coverage of the Ramsey case led to thousands of tips. Even years after the crime, members of the public regularly contacted the Boulder DA or BPD with information related to the case. Most was of no value, but occasionally something seemed promising.

For example, in 2005, a Boulder business owner called to report that a customer had left some papers with him as part of a transaction. Handwritten notes about JonBenét's murder were scrawled across the reverse side of the papers. Investigators from the DA's office followed up on the lead only to find the customer was an elderly man who was considering writing a book about the case. Tip after tip led nowhere. Still, potential evidence kept building, and by 2009, more than 60,000 pages of documents related to the case had been collected.[1]

John Ramsey said he refuses to give up searching for his daughter's murderer.

New DNA Evidence

At the time of the Ramsey murder, DNA analysis was still a relatively new technology. Over the next few years, advances allowed laboratory technicians to enhance the DNA sample from JonBenét's underwear to meet requirements for inclusion in databases. In 2003, police submitted the sample to the National DNA Index System (NDIS). The NDIS contains DNA from known and suspected criminals. It also contains DNA that has been recovered from crime scenes. Though the DNA from Unknown Male #1 was checked against millions of samples, no matches were found.

In 2008, Boulder district attorney Mary Lacy hoped further advances in DNA analysis could produce progress in the case. A method called touch DNA allowed investigators to examine JonBenét's clothing for additional sources of trace DNA. A lab found two such sources, one on the right side and one on the left side of the inside waistband of JonBenét's long johns. Both sources contained DNA that matched the DNA from Unknown Male #1. Lacy's office also ordered extensive testing to rule out contamination at the crime scene or during the autopsy as a source of the DNA from Unknown Male #1.

In July 2023, an online petition urging the use of forensic genealogy in the Ramsey case had more than 33,000 signatures.

Mary Lacy served as the Boulder district attorney from 2001 to 2009.

Lacy believed the evidence was strong enough to exonerate all the members of the Ramsey family. In a letter to John dated July 9, 2008, Lacy wrote, "It is very unlikely that there would be an innocent explanation for DNA found at three different locations on two separate items of clothing worn by the victim at the time of her murder. . . . It is therefore the position of the Boulder District Attorney's Office that this profile belongs to the perpetrator of the homicide."[2]

Critics of Lacy's opinion pointed to trace amounts of other DNA in both the samples taken at the time of the autopsy and the samples acquired from the long johns. They also speculated that the DNA might have been left in the underwear at the time of manufacturing. They argued that some of it could have transferred to the long johns when they came in contact with the underwear. However, subsequent testing to see whether new underwear would yield sufficient DNA for testing has not supported that theory.

Two Suspects Eliminated by DNA

In 2002, doctors discovered that Patsy's cancer had returned and spread to her brain. She sought care from the same team that had treated her during her first cancer battle. Her cancer went into remission for more than a year, but in 2005 it returned and spread aggressively. She died on June 24, 2006.

Shortly before Patsy's death, the Boulder DA's office informed the Ramseys that a new lead appeared promising and that they could expect a development in the case soon. That development came on August 16, 2006, when John Mark Karr was arrested in Thailand after confessing to JonBenét's murder. Karr had fled the United States after posting bail for a 2001 child pornography charge. Between 2002 and 2006, he corresponded via email with a University of Colorado professor. The exchanges eventually led to his confession.

After Karr's arrest, John issued a statement thanking the DA's office for their work. But hopes that the crime had been solved quickly collapsed. A close examination of Karr's emails revealed he had some of the details of the crime wrong. Upon his return to the United States, a sample of his DNA was tested. It did not match Unknown Male #1. Charges were dropped, but Karr tried to stay in the spotlight, appearing on multiple TV talk shows and maintaining a website dedicated to the crime.

Another false confession came in 2019. Gary Howard Oliva was a sex offender registered with the Colorado Bureau of Investigation and living in Boulder in 1996. Police arrested him

John Mark Karr was an elementary school teacher before he was arrested for possession of child pornography.

in 1997 after discovering a shrine to JonBenét in his home. However, his DNA did not match the DNA from the crime scene, and he was released. In 2016, he was sentenced to ten years in prison for possession of child pornography. While incarcerated, he corresponded with a former high school classmate. In one letter, Oliva confessed to accidentally killing JonBenét. The confession made national headlines, but police announced that they had ruled him out as a suspect years before.

John Ramsey Seeks Justice

John remarried in 2014 and moved to Utah. In 2021, he talked with Paula Woodward about his life since the crime. "After JonBenét was murdered, my will to live was definitely challenged," John said. "It was agony with that loss and pain. You try to make new memories and you do make new memories and those are good to fall back on and remember. But you don't get over it."[3]

John Ramsey said he kept talking about the case in hopes that it would prompt someone to come forward with a tip.

John has given several interviews appealing for more action on the case. He has accused the BPD of mishandling the case and failing to follow up on tips. In November 2022, the BPD responded with a statement saying, "Since JonBenét's murder, detectives have investigated leads stemming from more than 21,000 tips, letters, and emails. We have traveled to 19 states to interview or speak with more than 1,000 individuals. . . . As in any cold case homicide, the investigation can always benefit from the perspective of outside experts. So, in addition to talking with the private DNA labs, the Boulder Police Department will be consulting with the Colorado Cold Case Review Team in 2023."[4]

The Cold Case Review Team is made up of 27 volunteers, including investigators, laboratory personnel, forensics experts, and medical examiners. They meet four times per year and offer guidance as to how to proceed with the investigation of cases that have remained unsolved for years.

A Last, Best Hope

John has advocated for additional testing of the crime scene DNA, a request he included in a letter to Colorado governor Jared Polis in October 2022. Ramsey wanted DNA analysis done that would allow the crime scene sample to be compared with private DNA databases. Private databases are maintained by several laboratories offering DNA testing to the public for purposes of identifying genetic risk factors for medical conditions, revealing ethnic origins, and potentially finding relatives through a familial match. Familial matches occur when two samples are not an exact match but contain enough matching material to indicate a biological family relationship. A comparison of samples allows the labs to say how closely two people are biologically related.

Since 2010, consumers have been able to voluntarily add their DNA test results to a free public online database called GEDmatch to find additional familial matches. Familial matching has historically been used to help adoptees find their biological families or to identify missing persons or unidentified human remains. This familial matching led to the development of forensic genealogy. Some investigators have begun submitting crime scene DNA to private databases or GEDmatch to find familial matches. They then use the matches to construct a family tree. Factors such as age and location at the time of the crime and gender can narrow the pool of possible suspects.

Once a suspect is identified, investigators obtain a DNA sample. Samples can be collected from objects such as discarded clothing, used drinking straws, or door handles. Suspects may also voluntarily provide a sample or be served with a warrant compelling them to provide a sample. The sample is then compared with the crime scene DNA in hopes of obtaining an exact match.

The man who played Santa at the Ramseys' Christmas party was considered a suspect after pornography was found in his possession, but his DNA did not match that of Unknown Male #1.

After more than 26 years of no matches being found in the NDIS, John hoped that submitting the DNA profile for Unknown Male #1 to a private DNA database could produce familial matches, leading to the identification of new suspects. However, the NDIS does not use the same genetic markers as private labs, so a new analysis compatible with private databases would be required. The decision on whether to do such testing rests with the BPD, the law enforcement agency that has jurisdiction in the case. In 2022, the BPD announced it would not be pursuing an additional analysis, stating, "The amount of DNA evidence available for analysis is extremely small and complex. The sample could, in whole or in part, be consumed by DNA testing. . . . Whenever there is a proven technology that can reliably test forensic samples consistent with the samples available in this case, additional analysis will be conducted."[5]

John contended that such technology is already available, which is part of the reason he appealed for jurisdiction in the case to be taken from BPD and given to an independent agency. He turned 79 in December 2022 and knew time was running out for him to see justice served for his daughter. In his letter to Colorado's governor, he pleaded for the investigation to be seen through.

The Boulder Police Department regularly checks DNA databases for new matches to Unknown Male #1. John Ramsey hoped that someday his daughter's killer would be found.

"The murder of my daughter can never be undone," John wrote. "There will never be peace or closure. But there can and should be justice. . . . Solving the murder of my daughter will not fill the void in my heart, but it will identify and remove a demented and dangerous person from our midst and, in doing so, potentially protect the lives of other children. . . . As an elected leader, but more importantly, as a father, I respectfully ask you to do the right thing."[6]

TIMELINE

1996

- At 5:52 a.m. on December 26, Patsy Ramsey calls 911 to report her daughter, JonBenét, missing from their Boulder, Colorado, home.

- At approximately 1:00 p.m. on December 26, John Ramsey finds his daughter's body in a storage room in the basement of their home.

- At approximately 1:45 p.m. on December 26, the Boulder Police Department seals the Ramsey home and begins a homicide investigation.

- On December 27, an autopsy determines JonBenét's cause of death to be "asphyxia by strangulation associated with craniocerebral trauma."

- On December 28, John and Patsy Ramsey and siblings Burke, John Andrew, and Melinda Ramsey provide handwriting, blood, and DNA samples to police.

- On December 31, as JonBenét's funeral and burial are held in Georgia, the murder becomes the subject of national media attention, much of which suggests one or both of her parents are suspects.

1997

- On January 1, John and Patsy Ramsey give an interview to CNN and ask the public for help finding JonBenét's killer.

- On January 15, the Colorado Bureau of Investigation finds that DNA samples obtained during the autopsy do not match any family member.

- On April 18, Boulder district attorney Alex Hunter officially names John and Patsy Ramsey as the focus of the Boulder Police Department's investigation.

- On April 30, John and Patsy report for interrogations with Boulder law enforcement.

1998

- A grand jury convenes to examine evidence in the case. Burke, John Andrew, and Melinda testify, but John and Patsy are not called as witnesses.

1999

- After the conclusion of the confidential grand jury proceedings, Alex Hunter announces no charges will be filed due to insufficient evidence to prosecute any suspect.

2003

- Federal judge Julie E. Carnes issues a ruling dismissing a civil case against the Ramseys, stating, "The weight of the evidence is more consistent with a theory that an intruder murdered JonBenét than it is with a theory that Mrs. Ramsey did so."

2006

- On June 24, Patsy Ramsey dies of cancer.

- On August 16, John Mark Karr is arrested in Thailand after confessing to killing JonBenét in an email, but when his DNA doesn't match, charges are dropped.

2008

- Boulder district attorney Mary Lacy writes a letter to John Ramsey stating that new DNA evidence has exonerated all members of the Ramsey family.

2013

- A judge orders two criminal charges that were recommended by the grand jury in 1999 be made public, though the rest of the grand jury records remain sealed. The charges, identical for both Patsy and John, are child abuse resulting in death and being accessories to a crime.

2016

- The twentieth anniversary of the homicide sparks multiple books and television documentaries, including *The Case of: JonBenét Ramsey*, which supports the theory that Burke Ramsey killed his sister.

2022

- John Ramsey makes multiple media appearances and writes to Colorado's governor pushing for additional DNA testing that could enable the use of forensic genealogy.

ESSENTIAL FACTS

SIGNIFICANT EVENTS

- After initially being reported as a victim of a kidnapping, JonBenét Ramsey's body was found by her father in the family's Boulder, Colorado, home on December 26, 1996.

- On April 18, 1997, Boulder police publicly identified JonBenét's parents, John and Patsy Ramsey, as suspects despite DNA from an unknown male being found on JonBenét's body and clothes.

- After grand jury proceedings that lasted more than a year, Boulder district attorney Alex Hunter announced on October 13, 1999, that no charges would be filed in the case.

- On July 9, 2008, new DNA evidence led Boulder district attorney Mary Lacy to write a letter exonerating all family members.

- Since 2022, John Ramsey has urged police to use new DNA testing technology to identify new suspects.

KEY PLAYERS

- JonBenét Ramsey, a six-year-old living in Boulder, Colorado, was murdered in her home sometime during the night of December 25, 1996.

- John Ramsey, JonBenét's father, quickly became a suspect in the crime but later led efforts to persuade law enforcement to use new DNA technology to identify new suspects.

- Patsy Ramsey, JonBenét's mother, was also a suspect in the case and died in 2006.

- Burke Ramsey, JonBenét's older brother, was nine years old when his sister was murdered. Despite never being declared a suspect by the Boulder Police Department, several books and documentaries have accused him of killing his sister.

- Lou Smit, an experienced homicide detective, believed that an intruder killed JonBenét. He came out of retirement to join the investigation in March 1997. After resigning in September 1998, he continued to pursue leads until his death in 2010.

IMPACT ON SOCIETY

The killing of a young girl after Christmas in a quiet Colorado town both horrified and fascinated people around the world. JonBenét's beauty pageant participation and her family's wealth helped attract news audiences. The confusing evidence and police leaks provided additional material for tabloids and talk shows.

The Boulder Police Department, which made significant mistakes early in the investigation, quickly focused on JonBenét's parents as suspects. However, the evidence was never sufficient to bring a prosecution. New DNA evidence led a Boulder district attorney to exonerate the family in 2008, but skeptics of those findings continue to point to the family members as the killers. In 2022, John Ramsey began pushing for additional DNA testing, which he hoped would help catch his daughter's killer. The case has been the subject of multiple television documentaries, dozens of books, and hundreds of online forum discussions, podcast episodes, and videos, and it still makes headlines decades after the murder.

QUOTES

"This combination of wealth, attractiveness, the mystery of the murder and then the child beauty pageant angle made [the murder] a national and international story."

—Hilary Levey Friedman, a Harvard sociologist who studied the effect of JonBenét Ramsey's murder on beauty pageants

"It is very unlikely that there would be an innocent explanation for DNA found at three different locations on two separate items of clothing worn by the victim at the time of her murder. . . . It is therefore the position of the Boulder District Attorney's Office that this profile belongs to the perpetrator of the homicide."

—Boulder district attorney Mary Lacy in a 2008 letter to John Ramsey

GLOSSARY

advocate
Someone who works for the well-being and best interests of another.

allege
To assert an idea without proof or before it is proven.

asphyxia
Deprivation of oxygen that can result in death.

autopsy
An examination of a dead body to determine the cause of death.

bail
A fee paid by an accused person so they can be released from jail until their case has concluded.

conspiracy theory
A belief, without proof, that someone is responsible for an event or crime.

coroner
An official who investigates suspicious, violent, or sudden deaths.

craniocerebral
Involving both the skull and the brain.

defamation
The act of communicating false information that damages another person's reputation.

deposition
Sworn, recorded testimony given by a witness outside of a court, often in preparation for a legal proceeding.

district attorney
The primary attorney in a jurisdiction tasked with prosecuting crimes.

DNA
Deoxyribonucleic acid, the chemical that is the basis of genetics, through which various traits are passed from parent to child.

embezzlement
The theft of money meant for another purpose, often from the
perpetrator's employer.

exonerate
To clear someone of wrongdoing or blame due to compelling evidence.

forensic
Characterized by the use of scientific techniques to investigate a crime.

grooming
In cases of child abuse, a process in which a perpetrator tries to gain the trust of
and manipulate a victim.

indictment
A formal charge or accusation, especially in relation to a serious crime.

jurisdiction
A certain area within which a group has authority to make a legal decision or take
legal action.

libel
The act of knowingly publishing false information that damages another
person's reputation.

pedophile
A person who is sexually attracted to children.

perpetrator
Someone who commits a crime.

subpoena
To be ordered by a court of law to attend a legal proceeding or provide evidence.

voyeuristic
Obtaining pleasure or entertainment by observing the distress or misfortune
of others.

warrant
A court document allowing law enforcement to carry out an arrest or a search.

ADDITIONAL RESOURCES

SELECTED BIBLIOGRAPHY

Kolar, A. James. *Foreign Faction: Who Really Kidnapped JonBenét?* Ventus
Publishing, 2012.

Ramsey, John, and Patsy Ramsey. *The Death of Innocence: The Untold Story of
JonBenét's Murder and How Its Exploitation Compromised the Pursuit of Truth.*
Thomas Nelson Publishers, 2000.

Woodward, Paula. *We Have Your Daughter: The Unsolved Murder of JonBenét Ramsey
Twenty Years Later.* Prospecta Press, 2016.

FURTHER READINGS

Fleming, Candace. *Murder among Friends: How Leopold and Loeb Tried to Commit the
Perfect Crime.* Anne Schwartz Books, 2022.

Stevenson, Bryan A. *Just Mercy: Adapted for Young Adults: A True Story of the Fight for
Justice.* Delacorte Press, 2018.

Storm, Ashley. *The Casey Anthony Murder Case.* Abdo, 2024.

ONLINE RESOURCES

To learn more about the murder of JonBenét Ramsey,
please visit **abdobooklinks.com** or scan this QR code.
These links are routinely monitored and updated to
provide the most current information available.

MORE INFORMATION

For more information on this subject, contact or visit the following organizations:

ALCATRAZ EAST CRIME MUSEUM

2757 Pkwy.
Pigeon Forge, TN 37863
alcatrazeast.com

The Alcatraz East Crime Museum offers information about forensic science and investigative techniques for cold cases such as the Ramsey case.

DENVER PUBLIC LIBRARY

10 W. 14th Ave. Pkwy.
Denver, CO 80204
denverlibrary.org/content/denver-post

The Denver Public Library's *Denver Post* archive maintains a searchable database of articles from 1989 to the present that includes all *Denver Post* articles related to the Ramsey murder.

NATIONAL CENTER FOR MISSING & EXPLOITED CHILDREN

275 Lake Ave.
Rochester, NY 14608
missingkids.org

The National Center for Missing & Exploited Children provides resources and education to prevent child exploitation, kidnappings, and abuse.

SOURCE NOTES

CHAPTER 1. FROM MISSING TO MURDERED

1. Paula Woodward. "911 Call." *Paula Woodward*, n.d., paulawoodward.net. Accessed 6 July 2023.

2. Paula Woodward. *We Have Your Daughter: The Unsolved Murder of JonBenét Ramsey Twenty Years Later.* Prospecta Press, 2016. 23.

3. Charles Brennan. "Conduct Unbecoming: Inside the JonBenet Ramsey Case." *International Society of Barristers Quarterly*, Apr. 2000, isob.com. Accessed 6 July 2023.

4. Woodward, *We Have Your Daughter*, 21.

5. Michael Roberts. "Meet the Woman Living in Boulder's Notorious JonBenét Ramsey House." *Westword*, 4 Mar. 2023, westword.com. Accessed 6 July 2023.

6. Woodward, *We Have Your Daughter*, 72.

7. Woodward, *We Have Your Daughter*, 258–259.

8. John Ramsey and Patsy Ramsey. *The Death of Innocence: The Untold Story of JonBenét's Murder and How Its Exploitation Compromised the Pursuit of Truth.* Thomas Nelson Publishers, 2000. 523.

9. "John and Patsy Ramsey Tell Their Side of the Story." *CNN*, 27 Mar. 2000, cnn.com. Accessed 6 July 2023.

CHAPTER 2. THE INVESTIGATION BEGINS

1. A. James Kolar. *Foreign Faction: Who Really Kidnapped JonBenét?* Ventus Publishing, 2012. 246.

2. "Text of JonBenét Autopsy Report." *Denver Post*, 13 Aug. 1996, denverpost.com. Accessed 6 July 2023.

3. Douglas Zipes. "Can TASER Electronic Control Devices Cause Cardiac Arrest?" *Controversies in Cardiovascular Medicine*, 2014, ahajournals.org. Accessed 6 July 2023.

4. "Text of JonBenét Autopsy Report."

5. "Text of JonBenét Autopsy Report."

6. "Text of JonBenét Autopsy Report."

7. Paula Woodward. *Unsolved: The JonBenét Ramsey Murder 25 Years Later.* City Point Press, 2021. 65.

8. Paula Woodward. *We Have Your Daughter: The Unsolved Murder of JonBenét Ramsey Twenty Years Later.* Prospecta Press, 2016. 72–74.

9. "Lindbergh Kidnapping." *FBI*, n.d., fbi.gov. Accessed 6 July 2023.

10. Woodward, *We Have Your Daughter*, 81.

11. Woodward, *We Have Your Daughter*, 72–74.

12. Emily Willingham. "Forensic Experts Are Surprisingly Good at Telling Whether Two Writing Samples Match." *Scientific American*, 2 Aug. 2022, scientificamerican.com. Accessed 6 July 2023.

13. Woodward, *We Have Your Daughter*, 75–80.

14. Woodward, *We Have Your Daughter*, 273–274.

CHAPTER 3. THE CRIME SCENE

1. Paula Woodward. *We Have Your Daughter: The Unsolved Murder of JonBenét Ramsey Twenty Years Later*. Prospecta Press, 2016. 292.

2. Woodward, *We Have Your Daughter*, 150.

CHAPTER 4. INVESTIGATING THE RAMSEY FAMILY

1. Caitlin Flynn. "John Ramsey's First Wife Keeps a Low Profile." *Bustle*, 18 Sept. 2016, bustle.com. Accessed 6 July 2023.

2. Paula Woodward. *We Have Your Daughter: The Unsolved Murder of JonBenét Ramsey Twenty Years Later*. Prospecta Press, 2016. 92, 253.

3. Woodward, *We Have Your Daughter*, 86.

4. Phillip J. Resnick. "Filicide in the United States." *Indian Journal of Psychiatry*, Dec. 2016, ncbi.nlm.nih.gov. Accessed 6 July 2023.

5. Woodward, *We Have Your Daughter*, 208.

CHAPTER 5. PRESSURE BUILDS

1. Paula Woodward. *We Have Your Daughter: The Unsolved Murder of JonBenét Ramsey Twenty Years Later*. Prospecta Press, 2016. 160.

2. Woodward, *We Have Your Daughter*, 221.

3. A. James Kolar. *Foreign Faction: Who Really Kidnapped JonBenét?* Ventus Publishing, 2012. 129.

4. Woodward, *We Have Your Daughter*, 182.

5. Kolar, *Foreign Faction*, 128.

6. "New Funding Approved for JonBenet Ramsey Grand Jury." *CNN*, 5 Aug. 1999, cnn.com. Accessed 6 July 2023.

7. Kolar, *Foreign Faction*, 469.

8. Woodward, *We Have Your Daughter*, 356.

SOURCE NOTES CONTINUED

CHAPTER 6. THE INTRUDER THEORY

1. Tom Berman, Denise Martinez-Ramundo, and Muriel Pearson. "Who Killed JonBenet Ramsey? An Investigator's Dying Wish Keeps the Search Going with His Family." *ABC News*, 13 Jan. 2021, abcnews.go.com. Accessed 6 July 2023.

2. Patrick Nelson. "Deep Dive: FBI Estimates 500,000 Online Predators Are a Daily Threat to Kids Going Online." *KOAA5*, 2 June 2021, koaa.com. Accessed 6 July 2023.

3. Brenna O'Donnell. "Rise in Online Enticement and Other Trends: NCMEC Releases 2020 Exploitation Stats." *National Center for Missing & Exploited Children*, 24 Feb. 2021, missingkids.org. Accessed 6 July 2023.

4. A. James Kolar. *Foreign Faction: Who Really Kidnapped JonBenét?* Ventus Publishing, 2012. 155.

5. Paula Woodward. *We Have Your Daughter: The Unsolved Murder of JonBenét Ramsey Twenty Years Later*. Prospecta Press, 2016. 245, 391–392.

CHAPTER 7. THE RAMSEY CASE IN THE MEDIA

1. Paula Woodward. *We Have Your Daughter: The Unsolved Murder of JonBenét Ramsey Twenty Years Later*. Prospecta Press, 2016. 172.

2. Woodward, *We Have Your Daughter*, 183.

3. Woodward, *We Have Your Daughter*, 234.

4. Woodward, *We Have Your Daughter*, 399.

5. "JonBenet Ramsey: Investigating Mom." *Geraldo*. Investigative News Group, 31 Mar. 1997.

6. Woodward, *We Have Your Daughter*, 367.

7. Faith Karimi and Michael Martinez. "Court Papers: Grand Jury in 1999 Sought to Indict JonBenet Ramsey's Parents." *CNN*, 25 Oct. 2013, cnn.com. Accessed 6 July 2023.

8. Enjoli Francis. "JonBenet Ramsey's Brother Breaks Silence 20 Years after Her Murder." *ABC News*, 12 Sept. 2016, abcnews.go.com. Accessed 6 July 2023.

CHAPTER 8. DEAD ENDS AND LINGERING HOPE

1. A. James Kolar. *Foreign Faction: Who Really Kidnapped JonBenét?* Ventus Publishing, 2012. 218.

2. "DA Mary Lacy's Statement on Ramsey Case." *Daily Camera*, 14 Aug. 2009, dailycamera.com. Accessed 6 July 2023.

3. Paula Woodward. *Unsolved: The JonBenét Ramsey Murder 25 Years Later*. City Point Press, 2021. 159.

4. Dionne Waugh. "News Release: JonBenet Ramsey Homicide Update." *City of Boulder*, 9 Nov. 2022, bouldercolorado.gov. Accessed 6 July 2023.

5. Waugh, "News Release."

6. Audrey Conklin. "JonBenet's Father Challenges Colorado Governor to Meet: 'Time for Answers Is Running Out.'" *Fox News*, 30 Nov. 2022, foxnews.com. Accessed 6 July 2023.

ABOUT THE AUTHOR

RACHEL BITHELL

Rachel Bithell writes fiction and nonfiction for children, young adults, and their caregivers. Her favorite topics include science, history, and found families. When she's not writing for kids, she's usually teaching or playing with them. This is her fourth book.